Learning That
CLICS

Using Behavioral Science for Effective Learning Design

JANET AHN • MARY SLAUGHTER • JON THOMPSON

PRESS

Alexandria, VA

ATD Press is an internationally renowned source of insightful and practical information on talent development, training, and professional development.

ATD Press
1640 King Street
Alexandria, VA 22314 USA

Ordering information: Books published by ATD Press can be purchased by visiting ATD's website at td.org/books or by calling 800.628.2783 or 703.683.8100.

Library of Congress Control Number: 2022931447

ISBN-10: 1-953946-32-1
ISBN-13: 978-1-953946-32-4
e-ISBN: 978-1-953946-33-1

ATD Press Editorial Staff
Director: Sarah Halgas
Manager: Melissa Jones
Content Manager, Learning Sciences: Alexandria Clapp
Developmental Editor: Kathryn Stafford
Production Editor: Hannah Sternberg
Text Design: Shirley E.M. Raybuck
Cover Design: Rose Richey

Layout: PerfecType, Nashville, TN

Printed by BR Printers, San Jose, CA

Janet

I thank my parents, Bon and Dae Rheen, for always encouraging me to set high goals; my husband, Eddie, for being my rock; and my two daughters, Audrey and Everly, for being my biggest cheerleaders.

Mary

To my daughters, Lia and Ava. Thank you for the joy and steadfast love you bring into my life. You are the best gift imaginable.

Jon

I want to thank my parents, Mike and Helen, for helping me develop a love of learning; my brother, Ryan, for showing me how to have the courage to find my creative voice; and my wife, Christy, and daughters, Evelyn and Juliet, for their love and support and grace.

Contents

Contributor Sections

Standing on a Foundation of Continual Change

From the early planning stages for this book, we knew we were thinking differently about learning needs analysis compared with our past experiences. All three of us have held key learning leadership roles in various firms and have experienced firsthand the pressure to respond quickly to business leaders and market demands. We've also experienced times when learning was derailed, when it failed to meet learner expectations, or when it didn't produce the desired business impact. If you've ever found yourself in the position of defending why things didn't quite go the way you'd hoped, it's likely that some part of the needs analysis was either incomplete or ignored. The resulting business impact becomes lost time, wasted money, and frustrated colleagues—something none of us wants.

As we wrote our book, we became keenly aware of the temporal nature of work. We began our planning at least a year before the word *COVID* hit the news. Throughout the global pandemic, we worked together—mostly virtually—not only adapting our approach to collaboration, but also adapting the book itself to be as relevant as possible to the changing nature of work. In all candor, having a project like this was a gift that helped sustain us through the isolation and uncertainty that the global pandemic created.

It's now hard to imagine a world more complex. Overwhelming amounts of information, workforce reskilling needs, digital transformations, and emerging technologies seem to be the norm. It's not enough to simply talk about the speed of change, but the very nature of change is increasingly disruptive and often unexpected, coming in tsunami-like waves. We receive early warning signals that the wave is coming, but it's hard to fathom the real impact until change is upon us.

Our world is in constant flux, and it's not limited to business. Our cultural, social, and economic fabrics are rapidly being challenged and redefined, often driven by global inflection points like a recession, a pandemic, climate change, and trade wars. While all that sounds quite ominous, the rise of technology, micro-financing, and digital trade is accelerating, making it possible for a new, interconnected world of work to emerge.

A clearer sense of our humanity is also on the rise. Empathy. Compassion. How we treat one another, the values we demonstrate, and the behaviors we model not only are transparent, but also can circle the globe, literally with a keystroke. What once was hidden is now visible. What once was acceptable may crumble under the scrutiny of exposure and accountability.

Workplace Learning Evolution: Enablement Over Control

The days of linear, predictable, and stable content, controlled by a corporate learning function, have come to an end. It's simply not possible for any of us—no matter how talented, how experienced, or how smart—to forecast the future of what will need to be learned. The days of control are gone, and the world of enablement has arrived.

For at least the last decade, the learning industry has focused significant energy and investment on technology, looking for ways to shift learning from the traditional classroom to more personalized, mobile, and on-demand delivery channels. Technology platforms, smartphones, and robust apps have enabled major shifts in how we've begun to reimagine work. We often say, "Google and YouTube have changed forever the way we learn." There's no going back from our real-time, situation-specific searches that teach us what we need in that moment.

As important as those advances have been and continue to be, the next revolution in learning is turning inward to our own biology—the preferences, constraints, and needs of human psychology and the brain. The fields of social psychology and neuroscience have exploded over the last 20 years, yet much of the research has remained within the walls of academia and medicine. This research has given us a deeper understanding of how our brains register, process, encode, and recall information—the very essence of learning.

Our epiphany is this:

- Change continues to rapidly accelerate, with information growing exponentially.
- Learning professionals live at the heart of individual and organizational transformations.
- No matter how clever the technology, how talented the instructional designer, or how adaptive the facilitator, our profession can increase its impact if we factor in how the human brain learns.

Start by Reimagining Analysis

This book was written by learning professionals for learning professionals who aspire to become better at their craft. We've focused on applying science (for example, social and organizational psychology and neuroscience) to the profession of learning, starting first with reimagining what analysis is, and then reskilling ourselves to have science-based conversations with each other and the business leaders we support.

Historically, analysis has been the easiest step to hurry through or skip altogether, as we either accept someone else's definition of the "problem," or we assume the gap can be closed by training. In this book you'll learn about a new science-based framework called CLICS™, which is our acronym for Capacity, Layering, Intrinsic enablers, Coherence, and Social connections. These domains are based on five science concepts crucial for learning. Our goal is to share new tools that practitioners can immediately apply, building on their existing skill sets and methods. Additionally, we've intentionally designed CLICS to complement traditional methods of instructional design, be that ADDIE, SAM, or any other approach you may use.

About This Book

We begin in chapter 1 with an introduction to CLICS, describing the need to approach analysis in a new, more human-centric way. Then in chapter 2 we examine the underpinnings of the behavioral science of CLICS—how the brain works, learns, and applies.

In chapters 3–7, we present a deep dive into each of CLICS's respective domains along with practical applications. You'll learn about each domain and its relevant science concepts and models, then walk through three practical scenarios using the CLICS Tool. The intention is to immediately enable you to start using this framework when doing needs analysis with your stakeholders.

In chapter 8, we lay out the tool in its entirety and revisit one of our practical scenarios with a twist.

In chapter 9, we offer proven science-based techniques to apply during design and development to facilitate more effective learning outcomes.

Chapter 10 is our call to action for a learning approach that applies behavioral science insights to the world of work.

The appendix, "A Brief Tutorial on the Science of Testing Programs," provides straightforward guidance if you want or need to apply a rigorous approach to assessment. The process of measurement can be daunting, but consider whether this approach might be for you.

Throughout the book, sidebars containing interviews with business leaders (Cases in Point) and vignettes on the work of cutting-edge researchers (Scientist Spotlights) illuminate the practical side of these ideas.

So how should you use this book to get the most out of it?

- Apply the tool using a learning request you currently have before you.
- Reflect on how the scientific principles can help you guide conversations with your stakeholders.
- Identify questions to use in your own needs analysis that fit the domains but are relevant to your organization and circumstances.

To follow our work, or simply connect with us, please feel free to do so via LinkedIn:

- Mary: linkedin.com/in/maryslaughter
- Janet: linkedin.com/in/janet-n-ahn-phd-705b7796
- Jon: linkedin.com/in/jonthompson2758

We're so appreciative that you've chosen to read our work.

CHAPTER 1

Discovering CLICS: A Stronger Approach to Analysis

For today's learner, time and attention in the workplace, and in life, are at a premium. For organizations depending on those learners and the learning professionals tasked with supporting them, this is even more true. For those of us responsible for the design and development of learning, we've all probably heard something like this from our stakeholders:

- "Our people don't understand our new processes or what they need to do differently. Can't we pull some training together quickly?"
- "We need a new onboarding program that will make new hires proficient at their jobs in 30 days."
- "If we don't train people as soon as possible, we're not going to hit our sales targets. We need to start training now!"

If this sounds familiar, you're not alone. But, in order to actually help learners achieve lasting learning, it's essential to start at the beginning—how learning actually happens in our brains and is reinforced in our environment. This book provides the context, workplace examples, and supporting science that you'll need to approach analysis in a new way, using CLICS as a framework to guide your thinking, questioning, and assessment of the situation that may (or may not) require a learning solution.

The CLICS Framework

CLICS is a domain-based framework, grounded in social and organizational psychology and neuroscience concepts, that defines how our brains learn most effectively. The framework has implications across all phases of the learning solution process, which affects the overall learner experience as well as actual learning itself.

The primary goal of CLICS is to maximize the likelihood of sustained individual learning in an organizational context (Figure 1-1). Achieving this goal was the singular reason we created CLICS, with the five indicated domains, each underpinned by science foundations. The learner-relevant and workplace-relevant considerations help to balance the fact that learning solutions must consider both the audience for which they are intended as well as the environmental ecosystem into which they are deployed.

Figure 1-1. CLICS Framework

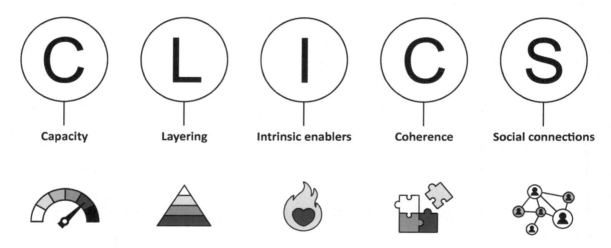

Relationship to Analysis, Design, Development, and Delivery

CLICS is intended to help learning professionals and stakeholders analyze the essential elements that impact how learning occurs in our brains and is reinforced (or not) in the environment—long before executing the design, development, and delivery of a potential learning solution.

In the analysis phase, our job is to ask questions that clarify the issues at hand. The goal is to not only define the root causes but also understand what the desired outcomes truly are. The starting point is a robust understanding of the needs of the learners as well as demands felt by stakeholders. The strong analysis creates clarity about what should be included in any recommended solution, whom it is intended for, and why they need it.

While this book focuses on the front-end analysis and definition of need, the CLICS framework is equally applicable when making decisions about the design, development, and delivery of learning solutions. Once in the delivery phase, organizations then have an opportunity to measure efficacy and impact, ultimately guiding modifications or confirming that we've created a solution that CLICS.

Broad Workplace Impact

At the core of CLICS is the recognition that learning solutions do not exist in a vacuum, and learning happens via structured learning events as well as on the job. Incoming information flows at an ever-increasing speed and volume, and it's often hard to distinguish the signal from the noise. That means part of the role of an effective analysis is to clearly define where learning is part of the solution, and not contribute to the "noise" by adding programs or content that don't positively affect the challenges at hand. In addition to being efficient with a learner's time, we should strive to set them up for success by maximizing the likelihood of real learning.

Within CLICS, the five domains connect and relate to one another as they examine the workplace context of how learning will happen, including the systems and environment into which learning should be integrated. Each domain considers both learner-relevant factors as well as workplace-relevant factors, because without both, the analysis would be incomplete (Figure 1-2).

Figure 1-2. CLICS Framework Considerations of Needs Analysis

No learning solution exists in a vacuum, so the environment into which that learning solution will be deployed is just as relevant as the content itself.

CLICS Domain Definitions

To get started, let's look at high-level definitions for each of the CLICS domains. Each domain will be described in greater detail in subsequent chapters.

Capacity

Capacity concerns the volume of information competing for the learner's working memory. Working memory is finite and can quickly reach capacity. When working memory is overloaded, extraneous information becomes "noise," requiring our brains to invest resources to look for the signals in the noise. Said another way, if everything is a priority, nothing is a priority. Capacity planning provides us with a clear set of parameters as part of the analysis, determining what is essential to retain and what might be considered optional.

A sense of overload can occur within a given learning solution, as well as from the external cognitive load being placed on the learners. For example, avoiding major training initiatives for tax professionals during tax season is a clear recognition of their capacity constraints that should be honored.

Layering

Layering concerns the optimal framing, structuring, sequencing, and repetition of concepts to ensure deep learning. This domain accounts for not only the sequencing of concepts included within the immediate need being analyzed, but also an understanding of related concepts the intended learners may, or may not, have previously encountered. Said another way, layering addresses the prerequisite knowledge that learners need before integrating new concepts.

Intrinsic Enablers

Intrinsic enablers are the motivating conditions required to enhance intrinsic motivation, to generate personal relevance and foster lasting learning. It's about finding those critical elements of value for the learners that cause them to flip the switch internally from being told to learn something to seeing the value and choosing to learn. Content that is relevant to actual job performance is typically embraced because of its intrinsic value to the learner.

Coherence

Coherence is the cognitive ease with which information fits together and amplifies related ideas. This domain incorporates the fit of concepts with one another as well as how the new concepts will relate to past learning experiences. An analysis sets the stage to ensure that the learners are not receiving conflicting guidance and that they understand any subtle nuances across competing ideas.

Social Connections

Social connections relate to the interpersonal support structure (be that physical, emotional, and psychological) necessary to learn optimally and to be effective. Analysis in this domain seeks to understand the skill or concept being taught, as well as what degree of social connection will help a learner absorb the new information.

To increase the likelihood of sustained learning, analysis in this domain seeks to uncover social opportunities to demonstrate and receive feedback when on the job, creating stronger emotional ties to the content itself.

How to Apply the Framework to Business Challenges

As learning professionals, we can experience many potential reasons why a stakeholder may come to us to define, design, develop, and deliver a new learning solution. Here are relevant examples of potential challenges that often trigger a needs analysis:

Situational
- Improve business results
- New business priorities
- New business tools
- Process change
- Compliance

Priority-Driven
- Answer on demand
- Enable professional development
- Drive change management

Competency-Based
- Broad skills
  - Leadership
  - Interpersonal
  - Compliance
  - Problem solving
  - Collaboration
  - Communication
- Technical skills
  - Tools
  - Role-specific

Role-Based
- People
  - Teaming
  - Coaching
  - Leading
  - Managing
  - Onboarding
- Tools
  - Software training
  - Physical tool training
- Process for "how to"
  - Do my job
  - Work with one another
  - Work with clients

CLICS Framework: Learning Analysis Question Tool

Throughout the book we will analyze three practical examples of where a stakeholder has asked the learning team for help. We'll use these scenarios to walk through the relevant questions from each domain of the CLICS framework.

We'll start by considering:
- The stakeholder's expressed need
- Characteristics of the intended learner population
- Sample questions to be asked and elements you'll want to consider as you evaluate the elements impacting each domain of the CLICS framework

Here you can see the structure of the CLICS Framework: Learning Analysis Question Tool, or CLICS Tool (Figure 1-3). Remember, during analysis, you're not yet defining a solution. Instead, you're gathering the necessary details that could support a solution. This is all about gathering information and defining the requirements of the challenge presented by your stakeholder.

Figure 1-3. CLICS Framework: Learning Analysis Question Tool

Domains and Science	👤 Learner-Relevant Considerations	👥 Workplace-Relevant Considerations
Capacity **Science:** • Finite working memory • Consequences of cognitive overload • Methods to enhance capacity	**How Much Is Sufficient?** *Solution balances how much information is essential versus how much learners can process, recall, and apply* **Core Questions** ❏ What outcomes are required to achieve success? ❏ Who are the essential learners to inform the learning requirements? ❏ How significant or complex is the necessary behavior change? **Additional Questions You Deem Relevant**	**What Will Compete or Distract?** *Solution considers competing initiatives and distractors to maximize learners' attention* **Core Questions** ❏ What other initiatives are currently planned that impact the learners? ❏ How will the organization prioritize the solution over competing demands? ❏ How could implementation be segmented to optimize learning? **Additional Questions You Deem Relevant**
Layering **Science:** • Schema acquisition • Spacing • Repetition	**What Structure Makes Sense?** *Solution integrates sequence, spacing, and frequency of critical concepts* **Core Questions** ❏ How will the new solution build on existing capabilities? ❏ What remedial support or incremental skills and knowledge are necessary? ❏ How much time will learners have to learn new concepts? **Additional Questions You Deem Relevant**	**How Does It Build on What Exists?** *Solution has purposeful connections to the workplace environment* **Core Questions** ❏ What related learning elements already exist? ❏ How capable are managers of reinforcing through feedback? ❏ What messaging will reinforce what has been learned? **Additional Questions You Deem Relevant**
Intrinsic enablers **Science:** • Intrinsic vs. extrinsic motivation • Relatedness • Competence • Autonomy • Self-concordance	**Why Will the Learner Care?** *Solution addresses meaning and relevance felt by learners* **Core Questions** ❏ How will the solution be relevant to learners? ❏ How might the solution feel rewarding? ❏ What level of autonomy will the solution support? **Additional Questions You Deem Relevant**	**How Are Intrinsic Enablers Promoted?** *Solution incorporates environmental prompts that activate learners' intrinsic motivation* **Core Questions** ❏ How will the solution align to the organization's purpose? ❏ How will leaders and managers reinforce the solution? ❏ How will the organization promote learner autonomy? **Additional Questions You Deem Relevant**

Domains and Science	Learner-Relevant Considerations	Workplace-Relevant Considerations
Coherence Science: • Associated network • Decoherent systems • Fluency	**How Big Is the Change?** *Solution associates new concepts with prior knowledge to promote adoption* **Core Questions** ❑ How does the solution fit with existing skills and knowledge? ❑ What context will help learners relate to the solution? ❑ How easy will the solution be for learners to understand? **Additional Questions You Deem Relevant**	**How Different Is the Desired State?** *Solution fits with, and is reinforced by, the workplace environment* **Core Questions** ❑ What leadership support is necessary to enable the change? ❑ What is different about the proposed change? ❑ What key elements in the workplace should change to support success? **Additional Questions You Deem Relevant**
Social connections Science: • Social learning theory • Social norms • Growth mindset	**How Will Connections Enhance Learning?** *Solution promotes interactions with others to help embed new concepts* **Core Questions** ❑ With whom will learners practice? ❑ From whom will learners receive feedback? ❑ How will learners be able to observe role models in action? **Additional Questions You Deem Relevant**	**How Could Connections Be Reinforced?** *Solution uses tools and processes to drive interpersonal interactions that activate learning* **Core Questions** ❑ What tools will learners leverage to interact with one another? ❑ In what ways will leaders encourage collaboration to accelerate adoption? ❑ How will successes and failures be shared? **Additional Questions You Deem Relevant**

Three Practical Examples

As we move into the individual chapters for each of the five domains of CLICS, our goal is to enable you to practice each element of the framework. We will share example scenarios that demonstrate how to apply CLICS to common, real-world situations.

In each of the CLICS domain chapters, we'll put the framework into action by exploring three common types of learning and change requests we typically face when serving the learning and development needs of our organizations.

These common situations will involve the following challenge areas:

- Situational
- Priority-driven
- Competency-based and role-based

Scenario 1 (Situational)

Improve business results: Revenue generation. Who has ever had a frustrated stakeholder come to them with the urgent request to create "training" to help improve performance and produce better results for the business? Chances are probably high that you have. Yet who hasn't wondered when this happens, "Is another course really the right solution?" Or, more to the point, "Are we even addressing the right challenge to solve the right problem?"

In this first scenario, your stakeholders are looking to improve business results and drive increased revenue. This common example usually comes with an existing assumption of what process or tool needs to be trained to drive those improved revenue results.

Additionally, these requests usually include some language like, "We really need you to train the <insert job role here> on the new process or tool next month, and have everyone up to speed with the new way of doing things about two to three weeks after go-live of that new process or tool."

Here are some company details. When working through this scenario in the subsequent domain chapters, it will be helpful to keep in mind some basic information about the company that will inform responses to the CLICS Tool: Core Questions.

Scenario 1: Company Details

Organization Type: Global products and services company

Employees: 25,000 worldwide

Footprint: Offices in North America; South America; Asia; and Europe, the Middle East, and Africa (EMEA)

Stakeholders: • Chief revenue officer
- VP of sales
- Product marketing business unit lead

The Ask: Your organization's sales figures are not meeting projections, so the three stakeholders ask you to design and deploy training on some revised approaches to selling (such as moving from transactional-based selling to relational-based selling) and some new sales software to better manage the process.

Scenario 2 (Priority-Driven)

Change management: Hybrid work. For many years, the idea of "work where you are" has been a common theme for workforce and workplace planning. The global pandemic accelerated efforts to move toward the formalization of policies and procedures that support working models where an employee may not be physically colocated with peers in the same office or even in the same city.

These new ways of working drive significant and broad-reaching change throughout an organization with potential impacts not only on how employees work with one another, but on how they serve their clients. Potential changes connected to hybrid work models are more relevant than ever.

In the second scenario, you'll encounter a priority-driven example of change within an organization. Stakeholders have approached HR requesting training to prepare employees for a new way of working. This is a broad-reaching situation affecting multiple roles throughout the organization, requiring upskilling for the systems and procedures that will make such a change possible.

Change initiatives with as broad a scope as this can quickly become unmanageable as the scope balloons to capture more requirements and audiences. In these situations, it is more important than ever to keep watch on the dependencies and connections between systems, processes, and people to ensure cohesive planning and communications from end to end.

Scenario 2: Company Details

Organization Type: National consumer products company

Employees: 60,000 nationally across the US

Footprint: Offices in New York, Atlanta, Dallas, Salt Lake City, and Los Angeles, and other facilities spread regionally

Stakeholders:
- Chief operations officer
- Chief HR officer
- Chief information officer
- Business unit leads

The Ask: Your organization is looking to enable hybrid ways of working following recent office closures due to the COVID-19 pandemic, as well as achieve long-term goals of enabling future-focused strategies of the workforce. As a result, training and change management is needed on new systems, processes, and behaviors among employees, as well as on how to interact with clients.

Scenario 3 (Competency- or Role-Based)

New leadership development: Inclusivity. We hear just about every day the words *diversity* and *inclusion,* so much it can be easy to confuse the two, but each has a distinct difference. Khalil Smith, Akamai Technologies' Vice President of Inclusion, Diversity, and Engagement, said it well:

Leadership is synonymous with inclusion. Being able to organize others, listen to a variety of ideas, synthesize an optimal solution, and galvanize people to deliver on those ideas, is key to being a leader. At the core of those behaviors is an authentic, deliberate, and unyielding commitment to inclusion. If a leader is ignoring the will and input of those around them, they are missing out on some of the most powerful and sustainable elements of leadership, and are instead relying on brute force, fear, coercion, or a misguided belief that they alone have the best and most complete answers to increasingly complex and multi-faceted problems (Ahn 2021).

Corporate diversity, equity, and inclusion efforts have now expanded to include belonging—a sense of fit, alignment, and psychological safety. Seeking other's perspectives and understanding differences increases the likelihood of authentic and actionable inclusion. The price of ignoring this is increased voluntary attrition, or even worse, people who quit and stay.

In the third scenario, you'll be stepping in as an L&D professional with a global financial services organization. Historically, there has been a positive history of diverse representation, given the mix of the workforce in the organization's offices and its global presence. However, current events have brought the organization to an inflection point, and the CEO and board want to examine the organization's values and practices to ensure inclusive practices are in place. This will mean a complete update of all leadership curricula to account for the new focus.

In addition, you'll be supporting the newly hired chief diversity officer as she plans and implements an overhaul of the current organizational values through the lens of diversity, equity, and inclusion. This will include learning to support any new systems and processes that emerge as part of the changes.

Scenario 3: Company Details

Organization Type: Global financial services

Employees: 100,000 globally

Footprint: Offices in North America; South America; Europe, Middle East, and Africa (EMEA)

Stakeholders:
- Chief executive officer
- Chief talent officer
- Chief diversity officer (newly hired)
- Board of directors

The Ask: Your organization is looking to support and empower broadscale updates to its corporate values in support of current DEI realities. The objective, and hope, of your stakeholders is to help the organization to attract and retain the top talent in the world around financial services. This includes the recent hiring of a chief diversity officer, who will be leading the delivery of this mandate from the CEO and board of directors.

Looking Ahead

Now you have an understanding of the CLICS framework and are ready to see how we apply the five domains in chapters 3 through 7. First, though, we will review some of the foundational scientific concepts behind CLICS and why its considerations should matter to you.

CHAPTER 2

Our Brains and the Science of Learning

The goal for learning professionals is to help people retain information in the best way possible. Although everyone learns differently and uniquely, there are basic principles that learning professionals should be aware of to maximize people's potential. This chapter reviews those basic principles, structured in terms of how the brain works, learns, and applies.

Keeping these principles in mind during the analysis phase can advance learning. We do not claim these principles are exhaustive or comprehensive, but we do view them as guardrails that will keep you on track during the analysis phase. We present a deeper dive of these principles and how they relate to the CLICS model in subsequent chapters.

How the Brain Works

Tomorrow is the day. You spent weeks, perhaps months preparing for this workshop, where you will launch important training around inclusion and bias mitigation for the organization. You and your team have invested hours thinking, collaborating, and coordinating for this day. You have defined a series of objectives that this workshop aims to achieve. So, what can you do to ensure that valuable teaching doesn't all go down the drain? How can you ensure that people not only engage in the material now, but also retain the information and actively apply it on the job?

To start, it's helpful to know how people remember and retain information. How does the brain process events and record them as memories? In short, memory is an information-processing system that involves a set of processes used to encode, store, and retrieve information (Figure 2-1).

Encoding involves actively inputting information into the memory system. The brain processes, labels, and codes information it has received, then organizes it with other similar or relevant information, thereby connecting this new information to already existing concepts.

Once information has been encoded, the brain puts it into storage, or a permanent state of retention (long-term memory, LTM). For memory to go into storage, it must pass through the stages of sensory memory and short-term memory. Sensory memory is the very brief storage (up to a couple of seconds) of sensory events, such as sights, sounds, and tastes. We are constantly bombarded

Figure 2-1. How the Brain Processes Events

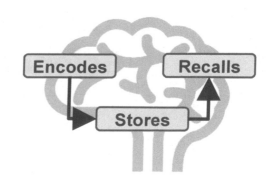

with sensory information that we cannot absorb and, frankly, don't need to. For example, what did you eat for lunch on Tuesday this week? If there was not anything unique about lunch outside of our daily rhythms and routines—for example, we didn't go out to eat with a friend we haven't seen in a while or we didn't contract food poisoning—the brain does not encode every detail. It is selective. Only some information, contingent on many factors (necessity, value, meaningfulness, and so forth), will move into short-term memory.

Short-term memory (STM), or "working memory," briefly stores incoming sensory memory. Exactly how much can be stored in STM? George Miller (1956) found that most people can retain about seven items in STM. Some remember five, some nine, so he claimed the capacity of STM as seven plus or minus two.

STM can be imagined as the information you just typed up on your computer—a document, a spreadsheet, or a webpage. Information at this stage can go in one of two ways: either to long-term memory (as if you saved it to your hard drive) or to trash (you deleted a document or closed a browser tab). For information to move from STM into LTM, it must be consciously and repeatedly practiced or rehearsed.

Otherwise, it will be forgotten.

Here is how quickly memory fades. Hermann Ebbinghaus analyzed how information is lost over time. He first memorized a bunch of nonsense syllables (for example, "WID" and "ZOF"), then measured how much of these he learned over different periods of time, 20 minutes to a month later. He then plotted his results on a graph, which became known as the "forgetting curve" (Figure 2-2). He found that an average person will lose about half of the memorized information after 20 minutes and 70 percent of the information after 24 hours when there are no attempts or strategies to retain it (Ebbinghaus 1885/1964). He determined that the speed of forgetting depends on several factors: the complexity of the material and psychological factors (such as sleep and stress). The best way to increase the strength of memory is through mnemonic techniques and spaced repetition.

Figure 2-2. The Ebbinghaus Forgetting Curve

The Ebbinghaus forgetting curve depicts how quickly retention of new information declines over time (Ebbinghaus 1885/1964).

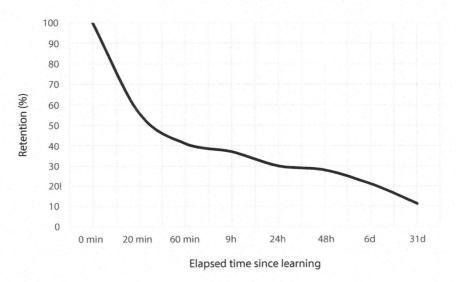

Finally, after doing the hard work to encode and store information, the brain must be able to retrieve it at relevant moments. Retrieval is getting the information out of memory and back into awareness. There are three ways you can retrieve information out of long-term memory storage:

- **Recall** is what we most often think about when referring to the retrieval process: it is when you can access information without cues, such as on an essay test.
- **Recognition** is when you identify information that you have previously learned after encountering it again. For example, you primarily rely on recognition for a multiple-choice test to help you choose the right answer.
- **Relearning** is exactly what it sounds like; it is learning information that you have previously learned. Imagine you learned French in high school but post–high school, you never really had the opportunity to practice it. Fast-forward many years later, and you are offered an opportunity to work in your company's Paris branch. Just for fun, you enroll in a French course online and are surprised by the speed at which you can pick up the language even after many years of not practicing it. This is relearning.

How the Brain Learns

Now that we know how the brain works to encode, process, and retrieve information, how does the brain then piece everything together? First, let's define what learning is:

Learning is a relatively permanent change in behavior or knowledge as a result of prior experience.

Learning is different from behaviors that are reflexes or instinctual (such as how birds build nests and migrate as winter approaches and how infants will naturally suck when their mouth is gently touched); these behaviors involve more primitive centers of the brain, like the spinal cord and the medulla. Learning, on the other hand, involves the higher-order structured parts of the brain like the cerebellum and the cerebral cortex.

In its most basic form, learning occurs when our mind automatically associates two events. That is, when two events occur closely together or in sequence, the brain learns if and how these events are connected through classical conditioning or operant conditioning.

You may have heard about classical conditioning before (also known as Pavlovian conditioning; a ringing bell causes a dog to salivate because it knows it's getting delicious food). Classical conditioning is when the dog links two events that repeatedly occur together. Classical conditioning is not just limited to how animals learn; we experience this associative process in our daily lives. For example, during a storm, your toddler might see lightning flash in the sky, then hear a loud boom of thunder that closely follows. She quickly learns to pair these two events, as lightning reliably predicts the impending boom of thunder, which causes her fear. So, by classical conditioning, every time she sees lightning, she will react in fear knowing that the booming sound of thunder will closely follow.

In operant conditioning, the association is made between a behavior and its consequence, either through reinforcement or punishment. A reinforcement consequence encourages more of that behavior, whereas a punishment deters a given behavior. For example, imagine you are potty-training a toddler. You verbally encourage and reward her with M&Ms every time she successfully uses the toilet. After repeated experiences, your toddler begins to associate the successful use of the toilet with receiving praise and chocolate treats. On the other hand, if your toddler is punished when exhibiting a certain behavior, she becomes conditioned to avoid such behavior (such as receiving a time-out every time she yells at her younger sibling).

Finally, observational learning (also called vicarious learning) adds a social layer to associative learning. We learn by watching others. What exactly are we watching? We watch how people act and speak and see how others respond to these actions and words, then eventually we imitate those behaviors and speech. Think of how a chimpanzee imitates gestures such as hand clapping or knocking on windows, or how an infant imitates their mother's speech and language. We tend to follow both positive and negative role models—or people who model both good and bad behaviors.

How the Brain Applies

How does the brain socialize the information it has registered, processed, retained, and learned? It highly depends on how (the degree to which and way in which) the brain is motivated. *Motivation* is defined as needs or wants that direct our behavior toward a goal. Although these needs and wants can be based on purely biological motives (such as hunger and thirst), motivation can also be driven by our psychological needs (for example, intrinsic versus extrinsic). Intrinsic motivation arises from internal factors that drive us to perform because of the sense of enjoyment and personal satisfaction we gain when we engage in those behaviors. On the other hand, extrinsic motivation arises from external factors that drive us to perform for the sake of gaining something else. It's a means to an end versus an end in itself (Figure 2-3).

Figure 2-3. Intrinsic Motivation versus Extrinsic Motivation

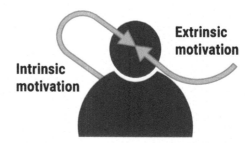

Intrinsic motivation emanates from within the individual, whereas extrinsic motivation comes from outside the individual

Think about why you're reading this book right now. Are you reading because you enjoy learning from it and want to use it to improve your approach to learning? If so, you're intrinsically motivated to engage here. But, if you're reading because your supervisor told you to or it's a necessary assignment, then your motivation is extrinsic. In reality, our motivation is a mixture of both these types, depending on context and situation; but, unsurprisingly, intrinsic motivation is linked to deeper and effective learning.

Whether individuals are motivated by intrinsic or extrinsic reasons, social norms can also be highly effective in reinforcing learning patterns. A social norm is a group's standard or expectation of what is considered appropriate or acceptable behavior—how a person should think, behave, and speak when in the group's presence (Deutsch and Gerard 1955; Berkowitz 2004). Social norms are powerful in their ability to shape and motivate behavior as clear roles, rules, and scripts are defined by the group.

Looking Ahead

In the next chapter, we begin a more detailed look into each of the CLICS domains, starting with Capacity. The subsequent five chapters follow a common structure of defining and presenting examples and support for the purpose behind the domain. Additionally, you will learn what the key considerations for the domain include, followed by a view of CLICS in practice in three real-world examples that span each of the five domains.

CHAPTER 3

Applying Capacity

There is a common idiom we use when we forget to do something: "It slipped my mind." Ever wonder how memory can literally "slip" out of one's mind? This will make a lot of sense when we understand how the mind works in retaining and retrieving memory—things can "slip" out! But how?

When we start to learn and acquire new information, we have very limited storage in what is known as short-term memory or "working memory." The amount of incoming memory we can store is what we refer to as "capacity." Simply put, capacity is the competition for working memory.

How to Leverage CLICS

In this chapter, we focus on the domain of Capacity (Figure 3-1).

There are clear consequences to overestimating one's capacity—feeling overloaded and depleted, increased levels of stress, and ultimately poor performance. What are some common signs that a workforce is stretched beyond their organizational capacity?

- Missed due dates and deadlines
- Increased errors in deliverables
- Rising levels of absenteeism and presenteeism
- Decreased engagement and motivation
- Increased turnover
- Less collaboration
- Signs of interpersonal conflict
- Decline in productivity

Figure 3-1. Capacity Domain of CLICS

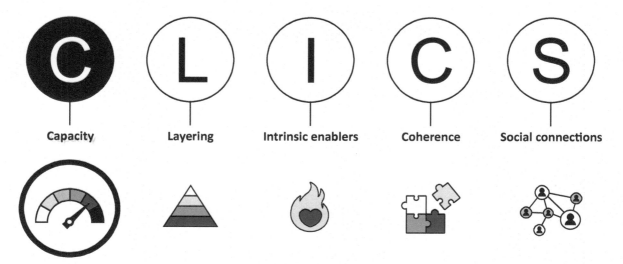

How to Assess Capacity in the Workplace

When considering capacity requirements of a planned learning solution, it is critical to plan for not only the capacity requirements of the learning itself but also the realities (or volume) of other activities that the learners must focus on concurrently.

An analysis of capacity should consider elements such as:

- Degree of difficulty of the new content
- Underlying assumptions about the learner's baseline skills and knowledge
- Related experiences or familiar context possessed by the learner
- A data visualization of competing organizational initiatives that require the learner's time and attention
- Existing workload and supporting processes (reporting, compliance, monthly or quarterly cycles)
- Spacing between major initiatives needed for integration and change management
- Time constraints imposed by business processes, laws, or regulations
- Resource demands and coordination with business units and corporate functions
- Feasibility of internally defined timelines for program design, development, and deployment, including access to subject matter experts
- The volume and frequency of task-switching involved in the new content being learned

Research Basis: Neural Capacity

Capacity can be understood in terms of the neurological basis and the cognitive basis. Neurologically, scientists have identified four main areas of the brain involved with memory:

- The amygdala is involved in highlighting emotionally charged memories like fear.
- The hippocampus is associated with declarative and episodic memory (memories associated with remembered facts and events), as well as the formation of new memories.
- The cerebellum processes procedural memories, such as learning how to ride a bike.
- The area that matters most for capacity concerns is the prefrontal cortex (PFC). The PFC is responsible for controlling basic executive functions, such as switching between mental tasks, monitoring, and updating information held in working memory, as well as suppressing some responses in favor of others.

The activity in the PFC is most crucial for consideration in the workplace because it is responsible for planning, problem solving, and reasoning. Executive functions and actions require motivation and self-control—all of which consume considerable resources and can overload one's capacity.

Even the most well-intended learning program will likely fall short of expectations when deployed in an over-crowded landscape. This often results from a lack of awareness of the competition for mindshare and bandwidth or weak internal coordination across organizational boundaries rather than a purposeful overloading of colleagues at work.

Curricula managers are typically quite good at thinking about the sequence and spacing of learning to achieve sustainable behavior change. But the reality is that competing demands for working memory come from across the organization, not just inside the learning team.

There's a range of predictable organizational actions that consume our limited cognitive bandwidth. We've all probably experienced many of the following:

- Restructuring or downsizing organizations
- Changing operations via a merger, an acquisition, or a divestiture
- Launching a new line of business, product, or service
- Opening a new market or geography
- Upgrading enterprise-wide technology or software platforms
- Tracking and reporting sales or other performance metrics
- Deploying new processes such as performance management, time tracking, or expense reporting

- Implementing new productivity tools that support collaboration and remote working
- Changing standards for end-user devices
- Managing predictable cycles such as performance reviews, compensation administration, or financial reporting
- Shifting the nature of work, such as centralized to distributed, in-person to virtual, or physical to digital presence

All these examples have one thing in common: They require the workforce to participate. As long as humans are part of the formula for success, any changes to technology, process, or workflow also will require some degree of behavioral change from the people doing the work.

 Research Basis: Cognitive Capacity

Capacity can also be understood from a cognitive aspect. John Sweller, an educational psychologist, formulated the Cognitive Load Theory, which refers to the limitations of working memory capacity to retain large amounts of knowledge at a time.

Sweller identified three types of cognitive load:

- **Intrinsic load** refers to the inherent level of difficulty or effort needed to understand or grasp content
- **Extraneous load** is the way information or tasks are presented to a learner (that is, fluency or how easily learners can process and register information)
- **Germane load** refers to work needed to process and construct a permanent store of knowledge, or schemas. A schema is a mental model or script that guides people in their thinking and doing—they are the basic building blocks of knowledge

Among these three types of cognitive load, Sweller distinguished which ones learning professionals have control over versus not. For instance, you can reduce extraneous load while considering ways to enhance germane load. This means material should be structured and presented in a way that is not distracting and difficult to process while simultaneously increasing ways of helping learners to connect new information with knowledge they already have via schemas.

How to Manage Capacity

Learning by its very nature is an attempt to change how we think or behave. The ideal approach is to begin by envisioning the desired learner experience. No one enjoys feeling stressed or overwhelmed at work, so part of the learning analysis should include an appreciation for the competing cognitive demands the learner will face. The research is clear—when our brains are overloaded or our energy is depleted, our ability to reason, recall, and adapt significantly declines. Clearly, the world of work is constantly changing, often as a response to emerging markets or environmental conditions. Nonetheless, if we can minimize foreseeable, competing cognitive demands, the opportunity to enable new workplace knowledge and skills accelerates.

Managing capacity seems logical, yet organizations passively ignore it all too often. A learner's self-diagnosis of inadequate capacity is usually accurate, and unfortunately it typically emerges when frustrations are high. In its simplest form, it sounds like, "I just don't have enough time." A lack of capacity may initially go undetected, as it's internal to the learner and is often masked by attempts to cope. Lacking the working memory to process information undermines attention, recall, and ultimately behavior change. Inadequate capacity leaves the learner asking a simple yet wise question:

If this is so important, why doesn't the organization make the time for me to actually learn?

Perhaps this workplace example of inadequate capacity will sound familiar.

I just don't know how I'm going to get this all done. Last week they launched a new learning management system, and earlier this month we also moved to a new project management tracking system. I'm still learning how to find what I'm looking for, not to mention entering data in a whole new way. It's now taking me two hours to do what used to take 20 minutes. To make it even worse, the cycle to refresh laptops starts next week. Don't get me wrong—I'm working on a five-year-old machine, so I'm ready for a new laptop. But the timing just seems poorly planned. And then today I got word about a new training curriculum being rolled out to the whole company. Ironically, it's about well-being and mindfulness. Just what we need—more training when everyone is swamped. Doesn't anyone at headquarters talk to one another? It's all too much.

Solid learning analysis extends beyond the learning design itself. It takes into consideration the surrounding environmental factors that directly influence the learner's ability to digest and apply what needs to be learned. Capacity is not outside the scope of analysis—quite the contrary. Having a comprehensive view of what the learning experience will be enables the organization to make better investment choices, both of time and money. Moving ahead without understanding capacity constraints is risky, as it can degrade the learner experience, which in turn creates reputational damage for the learning function.

Case in Point: Kimo Kippen

Founder, Aloha Learning Advisors, and former CLO, Hilton

Why is managing capacity such an important consideration?

KK: Most organizations are trying to push too much information all at the same time. Generally speaking, businesses suffer from too many organizational goals and need greater focus, because less truly is more. Everything flows from understanding organizational capacity. Unless you focus your efforts, learning essentially gets tossed to the workforce with the hope that something will stick.

What does defining capacity look like in practice?

KK: It all begins with aligning around the top business priorities and then focusing your limited resources. That step alone creates so much more success. Getting clarity on the WIGs—way important goals—clears the way for everything else. It grounds your learning efforts in operational discipline and minimizes the political whims and pet projects that naturally arise.

How do you gauge your success?

KK: Step one is getting to a manageable number of goals—the sweet spot is three to five. From there, you need clear business metrics (not just learning metrics) associated with those goals—like profitability, client satisfaction, and employee engagement. Another way of assessing success is in your processes. Are you staying focused on the most important priorities? Are you able to say no to things that would be nice to have but are not essential? Effective use of your resources—people, time, money—is another way to evaluate your success.

What did managing capacity teach you about your role as a learning leader?

KK: Acting as a broker of learning priorities is not enough, as it positions you as simply an order taker. Know where your work fits into the bigger scheme, including an appreciation for how the business makes money. Integrate your learning plans into business unit initiatives and their overall project management efforts to drive mutual accountability. Don't think of yourself as just supporting the business—you are part of it.

Research Basis: Capacity Limitations

An overload on capacity can cause learners to make more errors or experience some type of interference in the task at hand. Researchers have found that when learners are overloaded, they:

- Make more errors during problem solving because they are more distracted by irrelevant aspects of a problem
- Overuse unreliable mental shortcuts such as:
  - **Overgeneralization**—to extend beyond the available information
  - **Confirmation bias**—actively seek out information that confirms one's own opinion
  - **Anchoring bias**—reliance on initial impression of the first piece of information seen to make subsequent judgments

How to Expand Working Memory Capacity

Although as humans we are limited in our working memory and should be wary of capacity concerns, there are ways to help reduce load and increase capacity. The key is to enable fluent retrieval. In other words, use these strategies to make it easier for learners to process, retain, and ultimately remember new information.

There are four essential research-backed ways to expand working memory:

- Elaborative rehearsal
- Chunking
- Enhancing fluency
- Mnemonic techniques

Engage in Elaborative Rehearsal

One way to expand capacity is through elaborative rehearsal, a technique in which you connect the meaning of the new information to knowledge that is already stored, for example, schemas (Tigner 1999). Elaborative rehearsal is different from simply repeating information over and over to yourself—it requires deeper expansion and application. One way to engage in elaborative rehearsal is to learn the new information and "translate" it into your own words. What does it sound like and what are relevant examples that you are familiar with that you can apply? The more you can weave new information into old, or already existing knowledge, the more it will stick.

Chunk Information

In chunking, information is organized into manageable bits that help enhance capacity (Bodi, Powers, and Fitch-Hauser 2006). Consider how one can distinguish an expert from a novice; it's from the fluid and masterful way experts navigate and catalog their knowledge. Experts can chunk various discrete pieces of information into familiar patterns (Miller 1956). For example, researchers found that chess masters are able to chunk together several chess pieces in configuration according to their strategy. Similarly, experts in other domains exhibit this ability to chunk, such as in electronic circuitry (Egan and Schwartz 1979), radiology (Lesgold 1988), and computer programming (Ehrlich and Soloway 1984). In each of these areas, experts developed a sensitivity to patterns of meaningful information that are not available to novices, thereby enhancing their capacity and, ultimately, performance.

Enhance Fluency

Enhancing fluency is another way to expand one's capacity. Fluency is the relative ease experienced when learners process and register information. According to Alter and Oppenheimer (2009), "As a rule, every [cognitive] task can be described along a continuum from effortless to highly effortful, which produces a corresponding metacognitive experience that ranges from fluent to disfluent, respectively." Thus, for example, watching a film in a movie theater is more visually fluent than watching the same film on a small black and white television from the far end of a large room. One practical way of achieving fluency is via visual means. Think about a time when you attended a presentation and saw a slide that had so much text that it resembled the screen in the Matrix movies. Were you able to process that information well? Was it overwhelming trying to simultaneously listen to the presenter and read the information projected on the slide? Visual fluency helps enhance capacity.

Apply Mnemonic Techniques

Mnemonic devices are memory aids that help us organize information to enhance capacity. They are especially useful when we want to recall larger bits of information such as steps, stages, phases, and parts of a system (Bellezza 1981). Think about how one remembers the colors of a rainbow (Roy G. Biv) or the spelling of *arithmetic* (a rat in the house might eat the ice cream). Mnemonics assist memory to further enhance capacity.

Scientist Spotlight: Tessa West, PhD
Professor, New York University; Author; Consultant

The experience of "cognitive overload"—feeling like you don't have the mental resources to cope with the demands of the situation—is in the air these days. Seventy-two percent of managers felt more pressure to deliver during the pandemic than before it, despite having less time to get things done; more than half experienced routine burnout—the outcome of chronic cognitive overload.

Cognitive overload is bad for our mental and physical health, and it's bad for business. The critical question is: What steps can individuals and organizations take to reduce it?

First, kill task switching. When we task switch—toggle between writing an email, reading a report, and watching a meeting—we lose our ability to do any one task effectively.

Common wisdom suggests that those who can effectively multitask are the most productive at work, but the science shows the opposite; it takes us more time, not less, to get each of these tasks done. Leaders can model being present during meetings by not task switching themselves (no midmeeting emails!). Individuals can create calendars where time is chunked into one task at a time. No moving on to the next task until the first task is done.

Second, clarify priorities. People task switch when their bosses ask them to do three things and they don't know which one is most important, so they try to do it all at once.

Third, set clear work hours, no matter where you work. Hybrid and remote workers are at risk of cognitive overload from working all hours of the day. Creating explicit work hours is critical.

Cognitive overload is a ubiquitous experience at work. Following these guidelines can help reduce it, creating a healthier, more productive work environment.

Capacity: An Analysis Application Guide

Using the three example scenarios introduced in chapter 1, you will now walk through the analysis dealing with the domain of Capacity. You can also visit the book website to download an editable version of the tool and apply it to your own or any situation.

Working from the primary perspective of Capacity, our focus is first to identify specific considerations in the requirements from our stakeholders and how they will affect learners. Wanting to know what factors could affect learners, we ask, "How much is sufficient?" (learner-relevant) and "What will compete or distract?" (workplace-relevant).

The Capacity domain row from the CLICS Tool is extracted for reference (Figure 3-2). Before getting into the application of the framework using the tool, however, let's first look closer at what this row contains.

Figure 3-2. Capacity Domain of CLICS Tool

Domains and Science	👤 Learner-Relevant Considerations	👥 Workplace-Relevant Considerations
Capacity **Science:** • Finite working memory • Consequences of cognitive overload • Methods to enhance capacity	**How Much Is Sufficient?** *Solution balances how much information is essential versus how much learners can process, recall and apply* **Core Questions** ❑ What outcomes are required to achieve success? ❑ Who are the essential learners to inform the learning requirements? ❑ How significant or complex is the necessary behavior change? **Additional Questions You Deem Relevant**	**What Will Compete or Distract?** *Solution considers competing initiatives and distractors to maximize learners' attention* **Core Questions** ❑ What other initiatives are currently planned that impact the learners? ❑ How will the organization prioritize the solution over competing demands? ❑ How could implementation be segmented to optimize learning? **Additional Questions You Deem Relevant**

Learner-Relevant Core Questions

When gathering data in the Capacity domain regarding learner-relevant considerations, we begin with three core questions:

1. **What are required outcomes to achieve success?**
   This identifies and captures what the potential solution is really trying to accomplish, in terms of specific metrics or use cases of desired new outcomes, so we may understand the potential concepts necessary to achieve the stated requirements.

2. **Who are the essential learners to inform the learning requirements?**
   This identifies those whose behaviors and knowledge need to change, which will focus the amount of information needed to what is most relevant to achieve the desired outcomes, as well as provide constraints for the workplace-relevant considerations.

3. **How complex is the necessary behavior change?**
   This determines the degree of change required of the learner, which will guide how robust any potential solution needs to be to achieve desired outcomes.

Workplace-Relevant Core Questions

When gathering workplace data relevant to Capacity, we should consider what environmental conditions will surround learners and how the solution and information identified in the learner-relevant considerations will face competing demands.

1. **What other initiatives are currently planned that impact the learners?**

   This identifies competing sources of activity for the identified learners' attention during the delivery of any potential learning solution.

2. **How will the organization prioritize the solution over competing demands?**

   This identifies how attention and external support will be provided to the learners to complete and adopt the learning.

3. **How could implementation be segmented to optimize learning?**

   This identifies how concepts from the requirements could be potentially broken up and spaced in meaningful chunks to support effective learning transfer and manage learner capacity with other competing demands.

Beyond these, you may ask additional questions pertinent to your given situation, but the core questions are designed to capture the minimal amount of detail necessary to inform the design of an impactful solution based on stakeholder requirements.

Before stepping through the tool in three practical scenarios, keep in mind some of the common symptoms that your workforce is stretched beyond their capacity listed near the beginning of this chapter.

Scenario 1 (Situational)

Improve business results: Revenue generation. As a reminder, here is some high-level background for this scenario:

Scenario 1: Company Details

Organization Type: Global products and services company

Employees: 25,000 worldwide

Footprint: Offices in North America; South America; Asia; and Europe, the Middle East, and Africa (EMEA)

Stakeholders: • Chief revenue officer

• VP of sales

• Product marketing business unit lead

The Ask: Your organization's sales figures are not meeting projections, so the three stakeholders ask you to design and deploy training on some revised approaches to selling (such as moving from transactional-based selling to relational-based selling) and some new sales software to better manage the process.

Speaking with your stakeholders, you can direct your questions using the CLICS Tool Core Questions in the table (or download the interactive PDF from the book website and add your own questions based on a real situation you currently face).

Stakeholder Responses on Capacity

Review the answers your stakeholders have provided in the table.

Scenario 1: Learner-Relevant Considerations

Domains and Science	🙂 Learner-Relevant Considerations
⏲️ **Capacity** **Science:** • Finite working memory • Consequences of cognitive overload • Methods to enhance capacity	**How Much Is Sufficient?** *Solution balances how much information is essential versus how much learners can process, recall, and apply* **Core Questions** ❑ What are required outcomes to achieve success? *Success looks like our people are able to do their jobs well as measured by business development, total deal size and revenue, and, most importantly, repeat business* ❑ Who are the essential learners to inform the learning requirements? *All Salespeople* ❑ How complex is the necessary behavior change? *The approach to business development and selling, as well as the supporting software, are new and critical, but not too dissimilar to how sales works today. Potentially a reworking of skills and knowledge they should already have.* **Additional Questions You Deem Relevant**

Scenario 1: Workplace-Relevant Considerations

Domains and Science	Workplace-Relevant Considerations
Capacity	**What Will Compete or Distract?** *Solution considers competing initiatives and distractors to maximize learners' attention* **Core Questions** ❑ What other initiatives are currently planned that impact the learners? *Currently we're coming up on the close of both the quarter and the fiscal year end, so the sales team will be very focused on closing out existing pipeline deals and finding new ones. They also need to complete annual compliance training courses for the new fiscal year.* ❑ How will the organization prioritize the solution over competing demands? *The new approach and tool are fully supported by leadership and will be added both to onboarding programs for new salespeople and to programs upskilling existing salespeople as quickly as possible. Anything that will help the sales team achieve their sales metrics will be welcomed.* ❑ How could implementation be segmented to optimize learning? *We want to deliver the new training to all salespeople at the year-end sales meeting next month. The current year results will be reviewed and new product strategies and offerings will be launched. We can do quarterly refresh sessions next year as well if needed.* **Additional Questions You Deem Relevant**

Capacity Debrief of Scenario 1

Given the answers and data collected, do you have any potential additional questions?

In this scenario, there are numerous red flags regarding Capacity, given its focus, that should stand out. Here are two of the most glaring:

► Missing Affected Learners

While the salespeople would certainly be part of the audience for any potential solution, there are numerous other roles typically involved with the overall sales process who would likely require varying degrees of access and exposure to any solution that affects the sales process and tools.

Those roles could include sales operations and fulfillment, technical sales support, client service and delivery, business development or relationship management, proposal response teams, and quality control or quality assurance functions.

Any of these additional roles that require elements of a proposed learning solution should be listed and included, especially when looking at schedules and events that compete for their attention.

☞ Planned Schedule: Insufficient Time

The current calendar indicates multiple events that can potentially compete for a learner's attention. Any proposed solution will need to account for these items from a timing, modality, and sequencing standpoint. For example, delivering a training solution at a year-end event (as the one described above) is doable, but given all the other activities occurring at the same time, it is questionable how effective this training can be to enable behavior change. The learners would have insufficient time to fully acquire and learn the material in a way that matters.

As you can see, the CLICS Tool gives you a structured way to identify and assess information within the five domains of the framework. What other questions would you ask to have enough information to begin designing a solution? We'll continue analyzing Scenario 1 in the next domain chapter, on Layering, but for now, let's move to another type of common request that learning and development professionals hear.

Scenario 2 (Priority-Driven)

Change management: Hybrid work model. As a reminder, here is some high-level background for this scenario:

Scenario 2: Company Details

Organization Type: National consumer products company

Employees: 60,000 nationally across the US

Footprint: Offices in New York, Atlanta, Dallas, Salt Lake City, Los Angeles, and other facilities spread regionally

Stakeholders:
- Chief operations officer
- Chief HR officer
- Chief information officer
- Business unit leads

The Ask: Your organization is looking to enable hybrid ways of working following recent office closures due to the COVID-19 pandemic, as well as achieve long-term goals of enabling future-focused strategies of the workforce. As a result, training and change management is needed on new systems, processes, and behaviors among employees, as well as on how to interact with clients.

Speaking with your stakeholders, you can direct your questions using the CLICS Tool Core Questions in the table (or download the interactive PDF from the book website and add your own questions based on a real situation you currently face).

Stakeholder Responses on Capacity

Review the answers the stakeholders have provided in the table.

Scenario 2: Learner-Relevant Considerations

Domains and Science	Learner-Relevant Considerations
Capacity **Science:** • Finite working memory • Consequences of cognitive overload • Methods to enhance capacity	**How Much Is Sufficient?** *Solution balances how much information is essential versus how much learners can process, recall, and apply* **Core Questions** ❏ What are required outcomes to achieve success? *We need to enable our people, and transform our operations, to function in a hybrid manner into the future. Hybrid means some people may be on-site, at company facilities, or at a client's site full-time; some may be remote full-time; and others may be some mix of both. This means finding ways to minimize the requirement for colleagues to be physically colocated.* ❏ Who are the essential learners to inform the learning requirements? *Everyone in the organization will be impacted in some way.* ❏ How complex is the necessary behavior change? *There's wide variation. For some people, this will be significantly different, and for others, much less so, as we have supported remote work in the past.* **Additional Questions You Deem Relevant**

Scenario 2: Workplace-Relevant Considerations

Domains and Science	Workplace-Relevant Considerations
Capacity	**What Will Compete or Distract?** *Solution considers competing initiatives and distractors to maximize learners' attention* **Core Questions** ❏ What other initiatives are currently planned that impact the learners? *This is a top-to-bottom transformation of the organization, and as such will need to occur alongside all normal, day-to-day operations.* ❏ How will the organization prioritize the solution over competing demands? *We will bring in additional support where necessary to accomplish the transformation and change management efforts. Additionally, leadership is committed to driving the change with messaging about priorities.* ❏ How could implementation be segmented to optimize learning? *The current plan is to push out new policies business unit by business unit, based on the styles of hybrid work relevant to each, with foundational change communication from corporate as well.* **Additional Questions You Deem Relevant**

Capacity Debrief of Scenario 2

Given the answers and data collected, do you have any potential additional questions?

This scenario deals with a large-scale change management effort with many moving parts and affected roles. Learning requests like this one tend to be like the tip of the iceberg, with highly relevant factors hidden beneath the surface.

As it relates to the Capacity domain, the lack of specific considerations in one area can lead to a lack of real clarity in the others, as follows:

► Target Learner Population Is Too Broad

Unlike Scenario 1, the issue at hand is not the omission of relevant learners—quite the opposite. The targeted learner population is actually too broad. While everyone in the organization may experience some degree of impact due to a hybrid work model, it is unlikely that everyone actually needs training on how to adapt.

Clearly defining the targeted learner population is an essential step in building achievable learning objectives. Without clarity about the learners, we run the risk of inaccurate learning objectives—either omitting important considerations or including unnecessary ones. Agreeing on the essential information is a precondition for anticipating and optimizing learner capacity. Uncovering and managing competing distractors and conflicting time demands are important safeguards for capacity planning as well.

What other questions might you ask your stakeholders here? Remember that you are really trying to uncover the scope of what is necessary for success. We'll revisit Scenario 2 in the next domain chapter, on Layering, but for now, let's move to Scenario 3.

Scenario 3 (Competency- or Role-Based)

Leadership development: Inclusivity. As a reminder, here is some high-level background for this scenario:

Scenario 3: Company Details

Organization Type: Global financial services

Employees: 100,000 globally

Footprint: Offices in North America; South America; Europe, Middle East, and Africa (EMEA)

Stakeholders:
- Chief executive officer
- Chief talent officer
- Chief diversity officer (newly hired)
- Board of directors

The Ask: Your organization is looking to support and empower broadscale updates to its corporate values in support of current DEI realities. The objective, and hope, of your stakeholders is to help the organization to attract and retain the top talent in the world around financial services. This includes the recent hiring of a chief diversity officer, who will be leading the delivery of this mandate from the CEO and board of directors.

Speaking with your stakeholders, you can direct your questions using the CLICS Tool Core Questions in the table (or download the interactive PDF from the book website and add your own questions based on a real situation you currently face).

Stakeholder Responses on Capacity

Review the answers our stakeholders have provided in the table.

Scenario 3: Learner-Relevant Considerations

Domains and Science	Learner-Relevant Considerations
Capacity **Science:** • Finite working memory • Consequences of cognitive overload • Methods to enhance capacity	**How Much Is Sufficient?** *Solution balances how much information is essential versus how much learners can process, recall, and apply* **Core Questions** ❏ What are required outcomes to achieve success? *We are seeking to transform our corporate values to make apparent the company's commitment to diversity and inclusion principles. In addition, the creation of our chief diversity officer role will include the need to transform our core leadership development programs to ensure we account for these new values in action as part of that curriculum.* ❏ Who are the essential learners to inform the learning requirements? *New values apply to everyone at the company.* ❏ How complex is the necessary behavior change? *The change needed isn't complex, but because the new values define a shift in cultural behaviors, it will be more significant for some than others.* **Additional Questions You Deem Relevant**

Scenario 3: Workplace-Relevant Considerations

Domains and Science	Workplace-Relevant Considerations
Capacity	**What Will Compete or Distract?** *Solution considers competing initiatives and distractors to maximize learners' attention* **Core Questions** ❑ What other initiatives are currently planned that impact the learners? *We're coming up on end-of-year pushes for quotas and reaching financial goals. Additionally, our annual leadership development cycle is currently being planned for next year, so we want to get these updates built into that curriculum before it is delivered.* ❑ How will the organization prioritize the solution over competing demands? *There is buy-in and support from the CEO and board of directors as executive sponsors. Also, the hiring of the chief diversity officer and the update of our organizational values and core leadership curricula are intended to demonstrate the top-down commitment to change.* ❑ How could implementation be segmented to optimize learning? *We'd like to roll out the changes to the values to the entire organization at once, and then make learning curricula updates to each leadership tier as appropriate.* **Additional Questions You Deem Relevant**

Capacity Debrief of Scenario 3

Given the answers and data collected, do you have any potential additional questions?

This scenario involves the high-visibility areas of corporate values and leadership development, both of which can be subject to interpretation and executive preferences. Terms like *values* and *leadership* are used. Through the lens of the CLICS Capacity domain, two areas need further exploration:

▸ No Identified Measures of Success

The stakeholder did imply financial measures, both revenue and expense, but there are no specifics about what that really means. It also appears as though the plan is to update and communicate new company values to leaders and support the adoption of diversity initiatives promoted by the new chief diversity officer. Overall, there's a lot missing regarding desired outcomes, which in turn impact capacity. How will success be measured? Is it behavioral changes? Or are there quantitative metrics that are expected but not yet expressed?

▸ Understated Level of Complexity

If they haven't clearly articulated the desired outcomes and measures of success, then it's hard to validate that "the change needed isn't complex" or that "it will be more significant for some than others." Given the global footprint of the organization, the change of values and renewed emphasis on inclusion will have varying impact across geographies and cultures. These nuances will make the effort required to embed desired behaviors variable from one location to another. It is likely that localization will be needed not only for the updated leadership development programs but also for the change management process itself.

Understanding the complexity of the desired change means having accurate information about the who, why, what, and how to accurately gauge the impact on learner capacity.

We'll revisit Scenario 3 in chapter 4 on the Layering domain. Next, let's review some key takeaways from the Capacity domain when using CLICS to analyze your stakeholders' requests.

 Key Takeaways: Capacity

- Capacity: The volume of information competing for the learner's working memory
- Relevant science concepts
  - Finite working memory
  - Consequences of capacity
  - Methods to improve memory and retention
- Analysis in action
  - Clearly define learning objectives and metrics
  - Validate essential audience and stakeholder requirements
  - Confirm leadership buy-in and the support they will provide

CHAPTER 4
Applying Layering

If you've ever constructed anything with Legos, you know that each block needs to be correctly sequenced to fit within the existing structure. If not, you soon will discover that the final product won't look right, and in some cases, you can't even continue building.

Layering is the brain's cognitive version of working with Legos. It's the optimal framing, structuring, sequencing, and repetition of concepts to ensure deep learning. People don't learn in discrete and disjointed ways. Effective learning is actively constructed and built upon existing mental models (schemas). Layering means creating the connective tissue between new ideas and existing knowledge to ensure the smooth acquisition of new skills or concepts.

How to Leverage CLICS

In this chapter, we focus on the domain of Layering (Figure 4-1).

Layering matters because of how the brain learns new information. It acquires different schemas via association. In essence, the brain learns by layering new schemas onto preexisting ones, creating relevance and meaning.

Figure 4-1. Layering Domain of CLICS

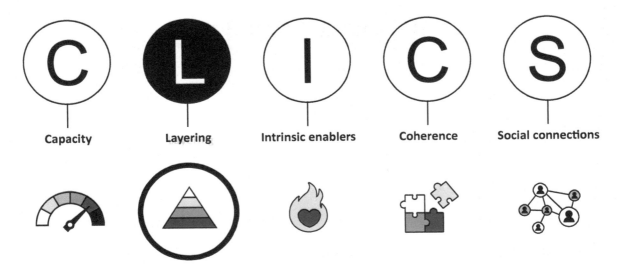

 Research Basis: Schema Acquisition

The basic building blocks of knowledge are known as schemas. Schemas are mental models that guide people in their thinking and doing. When people learn new information, they adjust their schemas through two processes: assimilation and accommodation.

People can assimilate new information or experiences in terms of their existing schemas—that is, they take in new information and assimilate it to what they already know. Or, they can accommodate new information and change their schemas accordingly. For example, imagine a toddler (Milly) has an existing schema for dogs because her family owns a poodle. When Milly sees other dog breeds (for example, a beagle) at the park, she says, "Look, a dog!" This indicates that she has assimilated the "beagle" concept into her already existing dog schema.

But one day, Milly encounters a cat for the first time and says, "Look, a dog!" Having the basic schema that a dog is an animal with fur and four legs, Milly automatically labels all furry, four-legged animals as dogs. When Milly's caregiver tells her that the animal she encountered is actually not a dog but a cat, Milly must accommodate her schema for dogs to include more information based on her recent experience (that is, dogs are furry, have four legs, and have longer snouts). Milly's schema for dog was too broad, so she now has to modify and adjust her schema for dogs and form a new one for cats.

How to Assess Layering in the Workplace

Analyzing layering is slightly more difficult than capacity analysis, as the workforce impacts are less obvious. When a person is overwhelmed and unable to process any more information or assimilate any more tasks, the self-diagnosis is pretty accurate: "I just can't handle any more."

The analysis of how information is layered in an organization means examining communication patterns such as sequencing, frequency, spacing, and reinforcement. The goal of layering is to enable concepts to build on one another, which in turn drives learner comprehension, retention, and on-the-job application. Remember, even the finest seeds won't germinate, take root, and flourish if the planting conditions aren't met.

When dealing with complex information or tasks, it's essential to pay close attention to layering. Work that includes highly technical information, strict adherence to safety protocols, or compliance with legal or regulatory requirements all demand layering in learning. Also, complex skills that need frequent, regular practice to perform at high standards must include a layering strategy. Examples of such skills are operating technical equipment, performing work in a hazardous environment, or interacting with others when exceptional relational or communication skills are required.

 Research Basis: Layering Structure

The way in which new information is structured has a dramatic impact on learning itself. Research shows that:

- Learning is enhanced when learners encounter consistent and repeated ideas across learning experiences (Bransford, Brown, and Cocking 2000; Bruner 1977, 1990).
- It is not enough merely to have repetition; the messages and theories should help learners make sense of their current experience. The types of messages should vary and not give contradictory signals, while remaining mainly consistent (Hammerness 2006).
- Engaging in repeated experiences with a certain set of concepts, combined with continual opportunities to practice relevant skills and modes of thinking and analysis, all support deeper learning and depth of development (Ericsson, Krampe, and Tesch-Römer 1993).
- If people learn in an environment that makes clear how ideas are connected and related, their understanding is deepened and their learning experiences are more meaningful. As Jerome Bruner (1977) argued, "Perhaps the most basic thing that can be said about human memory is that unless detail is placed into a structured pattern, it is rapidly forgotten."

Layering has relevance within learning itself, but it also applies to the business environment in which the learner will apply new ideas and skills. Prior to designing a solution, try using the checklist in Table 4-1 to ensure you've uncovered the variety of layering elements to incorporate.

Table 4-1. Recommended Checklist for Potential Layering Elements

Related Learning Content
- ❏ Courses, systems, and job aids
- ❏ Necessary prerequisites
- ❏ Sustainment mechanisms
- ❏ Learner's baseline knowledge and skills

Business Environment
- ❏ Learning in the flow of work
  - ◦ Degree of urgency and business impact
  - ◦ Expected job performance over time
  - ◦ Opportunity to practice and fail
  - ◦ Frequency of content use
- ❏ Ongoing operations and systems
- ❏ Tools, job aids, system prompts
- ❏ Access to experts and role models
- ❏ Managers with coaching skills
- ❏ Peers, cohort members, and mentors

What are the most common indicators that layering was absent from a learning solution?
- **Learner frustration**—lack of appreciation for existing skills and knowledge
- **Lower job productivity**—lack of appropriate context to make sense of and apply what has been learned
- **Disengagement**—gradual decrease in desire to find meaning in the midst of ambiguity
- **Unproductive failure**—recognition by learners that they are failing for reasons beyond their control, often related to weak onboarding
- **Lack of consistency**—lack of baseline understanding and context, fostering misunderstanding and misinterpretation
- **Formation of silos**—teams share workarounds and interpretations, fostering tribal knowledge
- **Increased confusion**—inadequate channels for clarifying questions or feedback

Here's an example of a learning scenario that didn't include planning for layering:

On the whole, I'm really glad I moved from sales to operations, but I must admit I feel completely lost after my first week of onboarding. I attended the training classes that were required, but at least half the time I didn't have a clue what they were talking about. So many acronyms and internal buzzwords—I never heard any of this in sales. I felt bad because I kept stopping the instructor to clarify terms, even though it was clear the rest of the class was not as lost as me.

By day three, I just started writing down words and phrases that I didn't understand. I figured I'd try to find someone on my team who could explain things to me once I got back to the office. Worst of all, when I started working in the software platform where we track our operational data, I kept screwing up the data entry, and I may have even sent the wrong file to my manager. I'm sure my report didn't look anything like the one built by the fellow next to me.

Why didn't they just develop a job aid that summarized the key reports that we have to create? Or better yet, it would be great to be paired with someone experienced so I could ask all my "stupid" questions without being embarrassed. I'm pretty discouraged, but I'll keep trying because I really like the people on my new team. I worry that I'm not carrying my load and others will notice. Do you ever feel like everyone else knows what's going on except you?

When layering is absent, learners will likely know something is amiss, but they may not be able to immediately identify what the gap is. Both the learners and those with whom they work might notice performance gaps, reduced speeds for task completion, and a greater need to ask for support from those around them. This is particularly true with new hires, as they are too often not provided with adequate layering in the new hire onboarding to fully appreciate the work they've been asked to accomplish.

Case in Point: Jesse Jackson, EdD
Senior Vice President and CLO, JP Morgan Chase

What is it about workplace learning that makes layering critical to deep learning?

JJ: Learning requires more intentionality today than ever before, as the workforce is overwhelmed and the workplace is rapidly changing. I think of layering as "surround sound," because it makes learning more immersive. Creating deep learning begins with meeting the learner where they are, which then allows you to guide them progressively to where you want them to be. Creating deep learning is like creating muscle memory, as both are reflexive in nature.

What does layering look like in practical application?

JJ: Layering provides a road map to move learners through multiple modalities and supports the multi-faceted ways in which people learn. Sequencing and repetition are important, but so is accessibility. Most of our workforce has grown up digital, which allows us to provide convenience and high-fidelity experiences through videos, simulations, access to experts, and curated content. These distributed modalities break learning into smaller, digestible bites that we can internalize and take back on the job for reinforcement. The more learning can be integrated into the work itself, the more opportunities for on-the-job observation, feedback, and behavior change.

In today's hybrid world of work, what advice would you offer on how to plan for the unknown?

JJ: Blended learning has been a reality for years, but the need for it was accelerated during the global pandemic. The same was true of digital transformations. They were already in progress but were accelerated by external events. We train more than 3,000 interns each summer and more than 20,000 new hires each year, so we have to be adaptive. This means not relying on any single supplier, expert, or modality. I'm sometimes asked about in-person learning, which I think still plays a critical role. It all begins with the purpose of the intervention. Transferring knowledge works well in a digital world and can be both effective and efficient. However, building culture and community works best in more proximate environments, as the social nature of this work is best fostered with in-person interactions.

How has your role as a learning leader changed over your career?

JJ: I've been fortunate to evolve our approach to governance, predominantly by laddering what learning does into the success of the business. I use the phrase "no hobbies" when talking with my team about internal client projects. That means we need to really understand and advise on what is being requested of us. What we do needs to impact the KPIs of the business, or else why are we pursuing it? The role of learning has never been more impactful, so having a clear framework for decision making will help guide investments toward the most important business drivers of success.

How to Layer Information

The ultimate goal of layering is to avoid what psychologists refer to as "extinction." The technical definition of extinction is the weakening of a learned association. More simply, when layering is not done well, the learner will unlearn what had previously been learned and ultimately forget.

There are three essential ways to approach layering to help our brains learn new information:

- Transfer of learning
- Spaced repetition
- Reinforcement

Transfer of Learning

To decide how best to layer, we need to first consider how learning transfers. *Transfer* refers to how existing knowledge influences current and future learning and how past learning is adapted to novel situations. One of the most commonplace but underrated areas where transfer occurs is career mobility. In today's talent market, individuals are looking for opportunities to grow and expand beyond their sphere, and similarly, organizations are often looking for new ways of thinking and developing. The intersection of these two goals is where you find talent that has very comparable experiences functionally but not necessarily similar industry experience.

The ability to transfer a skill set (such as business development) from Company A (oil and gas sector) to Company B (biotech or pharma) is a classic example of transfer—taking what you have learned about your field or discipline and applying it in a different industry. The core capabilities are similar even though the application is quite different.

Spaced Repetition

The idea behind spaced repetition is to give enough recovery time to absorb and digest new information before additional information is layered. As mentioned in chapter 2, Ebbinghaus suggested that information is lost over time (the forgetting curve). But information can be recovered with quick assessments and practice to mitigate forgetting. The use of spaced repetition has been proven to increase the rate of learning.

Reinforcement

For learning to occur effectively, the learning process must be repeatedly reinforced with multiple examples in multiple contexts and on different levels and orders of magnitude. One way to promote these concepts in repeated fashion is through reinforcement. You can use different types of reinforcements (positive and negative) as well as varying the timing of that reinforcement (schedules).

Research Basis: Reinforcement Types

The most effective way to teach a new behavior is through positive reinforcement. In positive reinforcement, a desirable or pleasant stimulus is added to increase a behavior. For example, you tell your toddler that if she eats all her vegetables at dinner, she will get ice cream for dessert. If eating ice cream is a strong enough incentive for your toddler, then you can expect her to finish all her broccoli.

You also can reinforce a new behavior via negative reinforcement. In negative reinforcement, an undesirable or unpleasant stimulus is removed to increase a behavior. It is important to note that "negative" does not mean "bad," and negative reinforcement is not the same as punishment. Think of "negative" here the way we think of negative numbers in math—a subtraction or removal rather than an evaluation of bad versus good. For example, think of how car manufacturers encouraged drivers to buckle their seat belts via negative reinforcement. The irritating beeping noise only stops when the driver manages to fasten their seat belt, thereby increasing the likelihood of displaying that desired behavior in the future.

Returning to the example of reinforcing your toddler's habit of eating all her vegetables: You can positively reinforce by giving her ice cream or you can negatively reinforce by taking away her favorite toy if she doesn't eat.

 Research Basis: Reinforcement Schedules

The timing or scheduling of reinforcements also matters. You can schedule very predictably (continuous schedule) or somewhat unpredictably (partial schedule). Researchers suggest following a continuous schedule of reinforcement early in the learning process.

For example, with a person new to a sales function, a continuous schedule of reinforcement would be most impactful. Following sales calls with clients, an effective sales coach should regularly debrief the usage of sales skills and the rep's ability to interact with the client. This could include building on what has been formally taught as well as skills demonstrated in previous client interactions.

Conversely, with a long-tenured sales professional, a partial schedule of reinforcement would be most effective. Feedback typically focuses on strong skills to be reinforced with fewer references to the gaps that a new salesperson would demonstrate. Adjusting the schedule of reinforcement to the experience of individuals is more effective for learning, but also more motivating for the long term.

Scientist Spotlight: Lisa Son, PhD
Professor, Barnard College; Author; Consultant

While spacing your study seems equivalent to massing your study—after all, the total amount of study time is equal—research has shown that for optimal long-term retention, spacing is the way to go.

You haven't done much studying all semester, and it's the night before your final exam. But you're not too worried, since you can just pull another all-nighter.

This scenario is too common. We cram our study into one long, uninterrupted session, usually hours at a time. And, our good grades tell us that these all-nighters might even work. At some point, however, we realize that this strategy—massing—is much less optimal than spacing, especially for long-term retention. We all know the experience of being able to recall information right now, but then forgetting that information after some time has passed.

It's not intuitive. Why would there be a difference between studying eight hours in short spurts across an entire semester versus studying eight hours straight? After all, you're devoting the same total amount of time to studying the material. But researchers have discovered that quality is more important than quantity. With massing, for example, you're unlikely to learn that you might forget the material. With spacing, the short breaks allow you to test yourself after some time has passed. Self-testing lets you know that you might not know, which, in turn, would be the signal for you to do something about it. These quality review sessions, which are interwoven into spaced study, can ensure deeper learning, going beyond your exam.

Layering: An Analysis Application Guide

Using the three example scenarios introduced in previous chapters, you will now walk through the analysis dealing with the domain of Layering. You can also visit the book website to download an editable version of the tool and apply it to your own or any situation.

After determining in the Capacity domain what and who best addresses our stakeholder requirements, the Layering domain focuses on how to structure a potential solution for greatest effect and impact. We identify considerations that affect learners by asking "What structure makes sense?" (learner-relevant) and "How does it build on what exists?" (workplace-relevant) for the learners in question given what they already receive to enable them.

The Layering domain row from the CLICS Tool is extracted for reference (Figure 4-2). Before getting into the application of the framework using the tool, however, let's first look closer at what this row contains.

Figure 4-2. Layering Domain of CLICS Tool

Domains and Science	Learner-Relevant Considerations	Workplace-Relevant Considerations
Layering **Science:** • Schema acquisition • Spacing • Repetition	**What Structure Makes Sense?** *Solution integrates sequence, spacing and frequency of critical concepts* **Core Questions** ❑ How will the new solution build on existing capabilities? ❑ What remedial support or incremental skills and knowledge are necessary? ❑ How much time will learners have to learn new concepts? **Additional Questions You Deem Relevant**	**How Does It Build on What Exists?** *Solution has purposeful connections to the workplace environment* **Core Questions** ❑ What related learning elements already exist? ❑ How capable are managers of reinforcing through feedback? ❑ What messaging will reinforce what has been learned? **Additional Questions You Deem Relevant**

Learner-Relevant Core Questions

In performing the analysis around the learner-relevant considerations, we ask three core questions:

1. **How will the new solution build on existing capabilities?**

   Identifies what the learners do or should already know versus how the new concepts build on existing knowledge.

2. **What remedial support or incremental skills and knowledge are necessary?**

   Identifies additional resources needed to close performance gaps that often result from inaccurate assumptions about existing skills or workplace support.

3. **How much time will learners have to learn new concepts?**

   Identifies the amount of spacing that could be incorporated to help learners comprehend and demonstrate the new concepts.

Workplace-Relevant Core Questions

When developing an approach for Layering, it is important to define the existing components that can be leveraged to support the design of the proposed learning solution.

1. **What related learning elements already exist?**

   Identifies connections between the proposed solution and existing learning that support the targeted change while also generating an inventory of current collateral.

2. **How capable are managers of reinforcing through regular feedback?**
   Identifies readiness of the managers to reinforce potential change in a way that improves the likelihood of effective learning.
3. **What messaging will reinforce what has been learned?**
   Defines opportunities to reinforce shared understanding and new behaviors that would foster sustained change.

Beyond these core questions, you may ask additional questions pertinent to your given situation, but the set of core questions are designed to capture the minimal amount of detail necessary to inform the design of an impactful solution based on stakeholder requirements.

Scenario 1 (Situational)

Improve business results: Revenue generation. As a reminder, here is some high-level background for this scenario:

Scenario 1: Company Details

Organization Type: Global products and services company

Employees: 25,000 worldwide

Footprint: Offices in North America; South America; Asia; and Europe, the Middle East, and Africa (EMEA)

Stakeholders:
- Chief revenue officer
- VP of sales
- Product marketing business unit lead

The Ask: Your organization's sales figures are not meeting projections, so the three stakeholders ask you to design and deploy training on some revised approaches to selling (such as moving from transactional-based selling to relational-based selling) and some new sales software to better manage the process.

Speaking with your stakeholders, you can direct your questions using the CLICS Tool Core Questions in the table (or download the interactive PDF from the book website and add your own questions based on a real situation you currently face).

Stakeholder Responses on Layering

Review the answers our stakeholders have provided in the table.

Scenario 1: Learner-Relevant Considerations

Domains and Science	👤 Learner-Relevant Considerations
Layering **Science:** • Schema acquisition • Spacing • Repetition	**What Structure Makes Sense?** *Solution integrates sequence, spacing, and frequency of critical concepts* **Core Questions** ❑ How will the new solution build on existing capabilities? *In addition to the new courses we want, our plan is to include a summary of changes based on the updated sales and business development process and tools comparing the new with the old to highlight where changes are being made.* ❑ What remedial support or incremental skills and knowledge are necessary? *We want to focus on having our people go through the new training and not bother with anything old. It's changing for a reason.* ❑ How much time will learners have to learn new concepts? *We're planning to deliver the new training during our upcoming annual sales meeting, which is a week in duration. We're carving out two of the five days exclusively for the training in the planned agenda.* **Additional Questions You Deem Relevant**

Scenario 1: Workplace-Relevant Considerations

Domains and Science	👥 Workplace-Relevant Considerations
Layering	**How Does It Build on What Exists?** *Solution has purposeful connections to the workplace environment* **Core Questions** ❑ What related learning elements already exist? *We should review existing sales process training courses to decide what content should be retained or perhaps retired.* ❑ How capable are managers of reinforcing through feedback? *Our managers currently provide ongoing feedback to staff based on the metrics we've previously discussed, so this should be a continuation of that process.* ❑ What messaging will reinforce what has been learned? *We have existing incentives and rewards built into our sales teams' compensation plans. We'll be amending these to align with the new process and targets and sharing as part of the rollout.* **Additional Questions You Deem Relevant**

Layering Debrief of Scenario 1

Given the answers and data collected, do you have any additional questions?

Looking at the responses and information gathered from stakeholders, a couple of critical gaps stand out:

► Unidentified or Unspecified Regional Differences and Needs

From the responses provided in the Capacity domain, the audience is inclusive of sales staff in global locations. However, there is no mention of how learner needs might vary across different regions within the company. It is being described as a global revision to the sales process, so there should be varied approaches from one region to the another. Specific linkages need to be defined by region between what is already in place and what is being introduced.

► Managers Unprepared to Support Necessary Repetition and Practice

The references to "business as usual" for managers should be considered a red flag. Assuming that all managers are qualified to provide meaningful support for the solution is shortsighted. Planning should include how to introduce managers to the new changes, including new behaviors, processes, and expectations.

Additionally, inaccurate assumptions about the current state can create challenges such as:

- Not enough sales managers to cope with the changes
- Sales managers lack the required coaching skills
- Regional variations regarding effective feedback have been ignored

Layering requires a logical order and sequencing of information, as well as how new information builds on what is already known. Layering enables learners to build the mental schemas necessary to internalize the solution. Within the sales domain, the opportunity to practice behaviors over time is foundational to embedding new skills. Any sustained sales behaviors also include enabling sales leaders to adequately explain the desired performance and provide ongoing feedback on skills development.

What other questions would you ask to have enough information to begin designing a solution? We'll look at more with Scenario 1 in the next domain chapter, on Intrinsic enablers, but for now, let's move to Layering considerations around a new hybrid model of work.

Scenario 2 (Priority-Driven)

Change management: Hybrid work model. As a reminder, here is some high-level background for this scenario:

Scenario 2: Company Details

Organization Type: National consumer products company

Employees: 60,000 nationally across the US

Footprint: Offices in New York, Atlanta, Dallas, Salt Lake, Los Angeles, and other facilities spread regionally

Stakeholders:
- Chief operations officer
- Chief HR officer
- Chief information officer
- Business unit leads

The Ask: Your organization is looking to enable hybrid ways of working following recent office closures due to the COVID-19 pandemic, as well as achieve long-term goals of enabling future-focused strategies of the workforce. As a result, training and change management is needed on new systems, processes, and behaviors among employees, as well as on how to interact with clients.

Speaking with your stakeholders, you can direct your questions using the CLICS Tool Core Questions in the table (or download the interactive PDF from the book website and add your own questions based on a real situation you currently face).

Stakeholder Responses on Layering

Review the answers our stakeholders have provided in the table.

Scenario 2: Learner-Relevant Considerations

Domains and Science	👤 Learner-Relevant Considerations
 Layering **Science:** • Schema acquisition • Spacing • Repetition	**What Structure Makes Sense?** *Solution integrates sequence, spacing, and frequency of critical concepts* **Core Questions** ❑ How will the new solution build on existing capabilities? *We are effectively providing more flexibility for work location based on the use of increased technology, so it should not be a great lift or change for employees from the current state.* ❑ What remedial support or incremental skills and knowledge are necessary? *Again, this new approach is all about greater flexibility enabled by technology improvements. We see this as a discrete set of new skills on how to use those new technologies. Connections between these new skills and current state are not necessary.* ❑ How much time will learners have to learn new concepts? *We don't see this as taking a significant amount of time for learners. We'd like to develop a series of self-help guides on the new technologies along with some communications on how to load them, why we're making these changes, and expected timelines. We'll roll this out across the footprint by division.* **Additional Questions You Deem Relevant**

Scenario 2: Workplace-Relevant Considerations

Domains and Science	👥 Workplace-Relevant Considerations
Layering	**How Does It Build on What Exists?** *Solution has purposeful connections to the workplace environment* **Core Questions** ❑ What related learning elements already exist? *Pieces of our current virtual meeting software will be kept, but we'll need to add new elements that support the integration of the virtual whiteboard and file collaboration features that we'll be adding into the mix.* ❑ How capable are managers of reinforcing through feedback? *Managers will be fine to manage this as it's just the use of new tools. Before the rollout, we will share talking points to promote the changes with their teams and colleagues.* ❑ What messaging will reinforce what has been learned? *We are working on a change communication campaign that will coincide with the launch of this new model. There will be some fun examples and rewards for teams that demonstrate and share their creative approaches to working in a hybrid model. The hope is that this fun approach will help to create an environment of trust that the new hybrid work model is endorsed and supported by the organization.* **Additional Questions You Deem Relevant**

Layering Debrief of Scenario 2

Given the answers and data collected, what additional questions might you consider asking the stakeholders?

Moving to a formal hybrid work policy does require the evolution of both attitudes and behaviors, especially those of managers and leaders. Based on the stakeholder responses to our questions, a couple of issues stand out.

▶ Disconnected Future and Current State: Local Considerations Missing

The responses from the stakeholders appear to be taking a top-down approach that does not account for localized variations. Different locations or work types (for example, production facilities versus office space only) will inevitably have unique needs that should be reflected in their policies, practices, and messaging. Additionally, differences in mass transit, traffic patterns, and even family school demands must be assessed, and are not reflected here. The absence of these details makes it much harder, if not impossible, to adequately define a new and effective hybrid work environment.

➤ Managers and Leaders Unprepared to Support the Shift

The belief that managers are prepared to support this hybrid work model is likely optimistic. There's no evidence that managers have been trained to lead in a new way, especially in setting expectations and providing feedback. Also, adapting patterns of communication to managing in a hybrid work environment is critical. Previous assumptions about organic, in-person communications are no longer valid, and new standards for messaging, including content and frequency, need to be established to support a successful transition.

Building on past experiences is, in itself, a form of layering, as it leverages existing contexts and schemas, making new information more relatable. Referencing existing tools and processes, and then bridging to future expectations, is an effective layering technique to enhance recall and promote behavior change that can be sustained.

What other questions would you ask to have enough information to begin designing a solution? We'll look at more with Scenario 2 in the next domain chapter, on Intrinsic enablers, but for now, let's move to Layering considerations in Scenario 3 around the new set of leadership values being adopted to account for an increased focus on inclusion in a global financial services organization.

Scenario 3 (Competency- or Role-Based)

Leadership development: Inclusivity. As a reminder, here is some high-level background for this scenario:

Scenario 3: Company Details

Organization Type: Global financial services

Employees: 100,000 globally

Footprint: Offices in North America; South America; Europe, Middle East, and Africa (EMEA)

Stakeholders:

- Chief executive officer
- Chief talent officer
- Chief diversity officer (newly hired)
- Board of directors

The Ask: Your organization is looking to support and empower broadscale updates to its corporate values in support of current DEI realities. The objective, and hope, of your stakeholders is to help the organization to attract and retain the top talent in the world around financial services. This includes the recent hiring of a chief diversity officer, who will be leading the delivery of this mandate from the CEO and board of directors.

Speaking with your stakeholders, you can direct your questions using the CLICS Tool Core Questions in the table (or download the interactive PDF from the book website and add your own questions based on a real situation you currently face).

Stakeholder Responses on Layering

Review the answers our stakeholders have provided in the table.

Scenario 3: Learner-Relevant Considerations

Domains and Science	Learner-Relevant Considerations
Layering **Science:** • Schema acquisition • Spacing • Repetition	**What Structure Makes Sense?** *Solution integrates sequence, spacing, and frequency of critical concepts* **Core Questions** ❑ How will the new solution build on existing capabilities? *Our plan is to announce the new values and retire the old ones simultaneously. We don't see any importance in focusing on what is going away. Instead we want to focus on the future direction in the form of our new values.* ❑ What remedial support or incremental skills and knowledge are necessary? *These are new values so we don't see the need to revisit anything they should already know. We envision the new values as being additive to our culture, making us more inclusive in daily practices. We don't see remedial support as being relevant.* ❑ How much time will learners have to learn new concepts? *We're planning a series of top-down communications as the foundational launch for the new values. Coupled with messaging will be training for our leadership ranks on how to put the values into practice.* *Additionally, we'll build the behaviors associated with the values into our performance management process to reflect what we want people to do. We estimate this will be a three-month program to roll everything out and get everyone up to speed.* **Additional Questions You Deem Relevant**

Scenario 3: Workplace-Relevant Considerations

Domains and Science	👥 Workplace-Relevant Considerations
Layering	**How Does It Build on What Exists?** *Solution has purposeful connections to the workplace environment* **Core Questions** ❑ What related learning elements already exist? *We have standard management skills for performance management, time reporting, coaching and mentoring, and employee relations. We see the new values messaging as just slotting next to those other pieces.* ❑ How capable are managers of reinforcing through feedback? *We will cascade the new values down through leadership ranks prior to the company-wide launch to prepare our managers to message and reinforce expectations around the new values.* ❑ What messaging will reinforce what has been learned? *We plan to launch a communication campaign to announce the new values. Additionally, we will send targeted messages to support the broader announcement. We are also planning to raise the visibility of our new chief diversity officer by having her lead a series of upcoming town halls throughout the company to promote and demonstrate leadership commitment to our new values.* **Additional Questions You Deem Relevant**

Layering Debrief of Scenario 3

Given the answers and data collected, do you have any potential additional questions?

In thinking through the Layering considerations for launching the new values, the stakeholders seem to have fallen short in two key areas.

► Unclear Connections From Current-State Values

The stakeholders seem to be over-relying on the impact of the launch itself. There's no context for why the values have changed or how the new values relate to the current ones. This approach will likely create a gap for learners to overcome, as they are left to interpret how to apply the values to their own behaviors.

► Lack of Planned Repetition to Support Long-Term Shift in Behaviors

The three-month timeframe misses the importance of repeated opportunities to observe, demonstrate, and receive feedback on demonstrating the new values. The planned approach omits Layering repetition almost completely. What about new hires who come in after the three-month rollout? What about remediation and further learning or practice when someone is found to not demonstrate the behaviors adequately? These are important questions to consider as well.

We'll revisit Scenario 3 in chapter 5, on the Intrinsic enablers domain. Next, let's review some key takeaways from the Layering domain when using CLICS to analyze your stakeholders' requests.

 Key Takeaways: Layering

- Layering: the optimal framing, structuring, sequencing, and repetition of concepts to ensure lasting learning
- Relevant science concepts:
  - Schema acquisition
  - Spacing
  - Repetition
- Analysis in action:
  - Determine the learners' baseline of skills and knowledge
  - Map out the ideal content sequence and where to add spacing
  - Verify the coaching and feedback capabilities of managers

CHAPTER 5
Applying Intrinsic Enablers

There is a saying: "Choose a job that you love, and you will never have to work a day in your life." It's simple enough to understand what this means: If you do what you love, then work won't feel like . . . well, work. Is there truth to this? For the most part, yes. When you are intrinsically motivated in your work, you work because there is inherent value in it and you derive personal gratification versus working because you are extrinsically motivated by compensation.

A video went viral of the music celebrity Lady Gaga early in her career. In it she spoke about depression and anxiety, which many people don't expect to hear about from famous people. She shared that by saying "yes" to too many things for the "wrong" reasons, she felt her love for music and performing slowly draining away. She learned that saying "no" to things that felt like obligations enabled her to say "yes" to things that felt right. In essence, learning to say "no" was an intrinsic enabler that fueled her passion and motivation as a performer.

How to Leverage CLICS

Intrinsic enablers are the conditions required to enhance innate motivation, generate personal relevance, and foster lasting learning. In this chapter, we focus on the domain of Intrinsic enablers (Figure 5-1).

Figure 5-1. Intrinsic Enablers Domain of CLICS

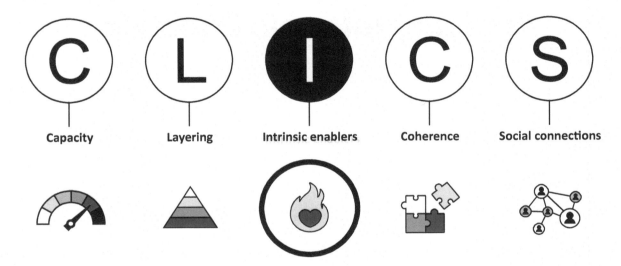

 Research Basis: Intrinsic Motivation Factors

In intrinsic motivation, an individual is driven to perform a task for its own sake and for internal rewards. An individual who is intrinsically motivated does something because they want to versus because they have to. There is inherent pleasure in engaging in a task because they enjoy it. On the other hand, in extrinsic motivation, an individual is driven to perform a task because of external rewards or to avoid punishment. An individual who is extrinsically motivated engages in a task as a means to an end—engaging in the task is not viewed as an end itself.

Unsurprisingly, intrinsic motivation, compared with extrinsic motivation, has been linked to greater engagement, learning, and performance.

How to Assess Intrinsic Enablers in the Workplace

To design learning that fulfills the learner's needs, the analysis phase should seek to uncover the potential motivators that the learners possess. These motivators are not always obvious and should not be assumed. Direct interaction with the learners is the best practice for seeking to understand what intrinsically motivates them.

With the increasing adoption of concepts such as mindfulness, well-being, and psychological safety, there's greater awareness than ever of how someone's mental state impacts their thinking, decision making, and behaviors. While intrinsic motivation is personal and internal, there are predictable patterns that can be externalized to optimize workplace learning. Factoring in learners' intrinsic motivation is also challenging because it is related to a sense of autonomy, which can be difficult for organizations to accept and promote.

Before designing a new learning intervention, the analysis should include an understanding of the learner's innate drivers. Their motivations might include the following.

Related to oneself:

- Experiencing growth and developing mastery
- Seeking autonomy
- Being heard
- Aligning with personal values
- Creating a sense of psychological safety

Related to others:

- Contributing or adding value
- Helping others
- Demonstrating capability to others
- Fostering trust
- Engaging in a shared purpose

 Scientist Spotlight: Paul J. Zak, PhD
Professor, Claremont Graduate University and Founder, Immersion Neuroscience

Extraordinary outcomes require discretionary effort.

While most leaders would agree with this statement, few know how to engineer discretionary effort by team members. My lab has identified the neural substrates of discretionary effort by measuring brain responses while people work. This has allowed us to determine the conditions in which people willingly exert extra effort at work.

Our findings can be boiled down to one word: Social.

Humans are social creatures and thrive in groups. When group membership is explicit, discretionary effort arises naturally to benefit one's community. Start with language. Direct reports are not your "employees" or "workers." Instead, call everyone a team member or colleague, or better a "genius" or an "artist."

Next, establish if colleagues are psychologically safe at work. Perceptions of danger drive people into singleton-survival mode rather than social-collaboration mode. Objective and consistent measurement and management of psychological safety is essential. Then, empower colleagues to experiment and try new things by creating a culture of trust. In high-trust organizations, mistakes are celebrated as learning experiences and discretionary effort is consistently and publicly recognized to establish community expectations. My group also discovered that discretionary effort is substantially higher when an organization's transcendent purpose is woven into all stages of colleagues' work. Transcendent purpose is an understanding of how one's work directly improves the lives of clients and society.

Social: language, safety, trust, and purpose. These are the foundations for discretionary effort and extraordinary outcomes.

Case in Point: Steven Sitek
Global Head of Learning, Gene Therapies, Novartis

What initiatives have you led to better understand learning at Novartis?

SS: We conducted a large-scale learning experience project that had a huge impact on how we approached our work. We wanted to understand not only how people took in information, but what would make the learning itself more compelling. Our goal was to remove the barriers and make the learner experience more integrated and appealing.

What were the most important intrinsic enablers you discovered?

SS: The closer we became to our workforce, three dynamics became clear. First, our colleagues had a deep curiosity to learn and grow their skills. Second, the pace of learning has accelerated exponentially over the last decade and the old assumptions about learning development and delivery were not sufficient, and in some cases no longer valid. Third, the volume of information is overwhelming, so we needed to leverage technology like never before.

How did you approach identifying those enablers?

SS: We literally shadowed our colleagues on the job, with the goal of deeply understanding how information flowed and how colleagues were motivated to learn. We wanted to understand in what ways they were dependent on access to people, time, systems, and tools. People who work in healthcare are typically intrinsically motivated and outcome oriented, so we never lost sight of being performance driven. We ultimately landed on three essential principles, "Accelerated, Amplified, and Integrated," as the keys to making learning compelling.

How has your role as a learning leader changed over your career?

SS: Certainly technology has impacted everything about the learning profession. Every day I encourage my team to strive for a consumer-grade experience, which means learning should be contextualized, personalized, integrated, and social. It's critical to reach beyond the boundaries of our learning organization. We should do everything we can to make learning a positive experience, including leveraging external partnerships and taking an interdisciplinary approach internally to support our colleagues. Our role is to fuel curiosity, drive growth, and enable meaningful impact, not just deliver learning.

Perhaps one of the best ways to determine when Intrinsic enablers are lacking is to ask the following questions. The answers will highlight the degree to which learners can personally relate to the situation and any potential learning solutions:

- Is learning driven by the need to comply or the desire to learn?
- How much monitoring is required for individuals to adopt new policies or skills?
- Do learners appreciate how the new content will help them achieve their goals?
- How aligned is the learning solution with the organizational values?
- Do learners persist in the face of challenging concepts or ideas?
- Are there clear, relevant connections to on-the-job success?
- Do learners demonstrate curiosity and seek related information?
- Why do learners avoid participating in learning programs?

Research Basis: Risk of Intrinsic Motivation Turning Extrinsic

Initial intrinsic motivation can turn into extrinsic motivation, also known as the overjustification effect.

Imagine Grace, a talented musician who enjoys playing with her band for the sake of creating music. She looks forward to every jam session in her bandmate's garage and even continues to practice on her own. She and her band offer to play for free at cafes, restaurants, and clubs, jumping on any and every opportunity just to play together. Until one day, when they are invited to open for a popular local band.

This event becomes the inflection point that takes Grace's band from no-names to headliners. They are now sought out. As their fame rises and gigs are regularly booked, acclaim pours in. But Grace starts to play only if she has to and starts spending less time playing in the absence of any external reward. What Grace is experiencing is the overjustification effect; her initial intrinsic motivation has turned extrinsic.

How to Promote Intrinsic Enablers

As part of the analysis process, it's important to define four factors.

1. Competence

Analysis focus: Desired performance and the degree of competence required.

Competence is about having the sense of self-efficacy and capability to complete a task. Think about a small child that has just learned how to scoot or ride a bike. The thrill of success will motivate that child to keep practicing and get better and faster just for the fun of it.

2. Autonomy

Analysis focus: Conditions that will allow the learner to work independently, as well as the level of independence required on the job.

Autonomy is where one feels in control of one's life and surroundings. Think back to being a teenager and being told you can't or should not do something and how much you resisted these constraints placed on you. This is a phenomenon called psychological reactance, which is the reaction you have when your freedom or autonomy has been limited or controlled.

3. Relationships and Connections

Analysis focus: Options for networking, collaboration, and creating interactions at work that enhance the desired outcome.

The desire to feel connected to and accepted by others is an absolute need. Think about one of the reasons being in quarantine and lockdown during a pandemic is so difficult—it cuts us off from the sense of belonging that is essential for survival.

4. Self-Concordant Goals

Analysis focus: How individual goals are aligned to the organization's goals and vision.

Self-concordant goals are those that reflect and fit who you are intrinsically. They express talents, interests, values, and potential that reside deep within your personality. People who pursue self-concordant goals are striving for goals that represent their core values versus goals that are situational.

When obstacles or challenges arise, those pursuing self-concordant goals will tolerate the ups and downs because their motivation is deeply sourced. We exert more energy and effort pursuing goals that are closest to our heart compared with goals that are extrinsically motivated. The more effort exerted, the greater the chance the goal will be achieved. The outcome of reaching goals increases the sense of competence, thereby increasing intrinsic motivation.

Intrinsic Enablers: An Analysis Application Guide

Using the three example scenarios introduced in previous chapters, you will now walk through the analysis dealing with the domain of Intrinsic enablers. You can also visit the book website to download an editable version of the tool and apply to your own or any situation.

The focus of the Intrinsic enablers domain is that to truly drive sustainable change, learners must connect with the change, and must want to internalize new information or behaviors. This comes by identifying considerations that impact them by asking "Why will the learner care?" (learner-relevant) and "How are intrinsic enablers promoted?" (workplace-relevant) to show how the organization values and supports the required change.

The Intrinsic enablers domain row from the CLICS Tool is extracted for reference as we walk through the three practical scenarios that follow (Figure 5-2).

Figure 5-2. Intrinsic Enablers Domain of CLICS Tool

Domains and Science	Learner-Relevant Considerations	Workplace-Relevant Considerations
Intrinsic enablers Science: • Intrinsic vs. extrinsic motivation • Relatedness • Competence • Autonomy • Self-concordance	**Why Will the Learner Care?** *Solution addresses meaning and relevance felt by learners* **Core Questions** ❏ How will the solution be relevant to learners? ❏ How might the solution feel rewarding? ❏ What level of autonomy will the solution support? **Additional Questions You Deem Relevant**	**How Are Intrinsic Enablers Promoted?** *Solution incorporates environmental prompts that activate learners' intrinsic motivation* **Core Questions** ❏ How will the solution align to the organization's purpose? ❏ How will leaders and managers reinforce the solution? ❏ How will the organization promote learner autonomy? **Additional Questions You Deem Relevant**

Learner-Relevant Core Questions

To perform the analysis for the Intrinsic enablers domain, we ask three core questions:

1. **How will the solution be relevant to learners?**

   Identifies job-related concepts that will motivate the learners to learn.

2. **How might the solution feel rewarding?**

   Identifies ways the solution activates learners' intrinsic motivation.

3. **What level of autonomy will the solution support?**

   Identifies the learners' expected level of flexibility and decision making embedded in the solution.

Workplace-Relevant Core Questions

To consider what exists in the environment around prospective learners and how learner-relevant considerations will impact the organization, we ask three core questions:

1. **How will the solution align to the organization's purpose?**

   Identifies how the solution balances learners' goals with the organization's purpose.

2. **How will leaders and managers reinforce the solution?**

   Identifies how those with influence foster a sense of relatedness and trust to support the solution.

3. **How will the organization promote learner autonomy?**

   Identifies the organization's desired level of flexibility and decision making on the part of the learners relative to the solution.

Beyond these core questions, you may ask additional questions pertinent to your given situation, but the sets of core questions are designed to capture minimum amounts of detail necessary to inform the design of an impactful solution based on stakeholder requirements.

Scenario 1 (Situational)

Improve business results: Revenue generation. As a reminder, here is some high-level background for this scenario:

Scenario 1: Company Details

Organization Type: Global products and services company

Employees: 25,000 worldwide

Footprint: Offices in North America; South America; Asia; and Europe, the Middle East, and Africa (EMEA)

Stakeholders:
- Chief revenue officer
- VP of sales
- Product marketing business unit lead

The Ask: Your organization's sales figures are not meeting projections, so the three stakeholders ask you to design and deploy training on some revised approaches to selling (such as moving from transactional-based selling to relational-based selling) and some new sales software to better manage the process.

Speaking with your stakeholders, you can direct your questions using the CLICS Tool Core Questions in the table (or download the interactive PDF from the book website and add your own questions based on a real situation you currently face).

Stakeholder Responses on Intrinsic Enablers

In the following table, review the answers our stakeholders have provided.

Scenario 1: Learner-Relevant Considerations

Domains and Science	Learner-Relevant Considerations
  Intrinsic enablers **Science:** • Intrinsic vs. extrinsic motivation • Relatedness • Competence • Autonomy • Self-concordance	**Why Will the Learner Care?** *Solution addresses meaning and relevance felt by learners* **Core Questions** ❑ How will the solution be relevant to learners? *The new approach to sales is intended to help make learners more productive, so that should make it very relevant. We're bringing in these new techniques to ultimately drive better revenue results.* ❑ How might the solution feel rewarding? *We hope that better results for the business tied to performance goals for the individual would make it feel very rewarding.* ❑ What level of autonomy will the solution support? *The relational sales approach and processes we are adopting are intended to help the salesperson connect with their clients. One of the purposes of this approach is to help the salesperson have more direct control over the approach they take with their accounts.* **Additional Questions You Deem Relevant**

Scenario 1: Workplace-Relevant Considerations

Domains and Science	Workplace-Relevant Considerations
  Intrinsic enablers	**How Are Intrinsic Enablers Promoted?** *Solution incorporates environmental prompts that activate learners' intrinsic motivation* **Core Questions** ❑ How will the solution align to the organization's purpose? *The solution should directly map to the relevant company goals that support serving our clients and achieving growth into the future. These linkages should be stressed as part of the training and change communications efforts.* ❑ How will leaders and managers reinforce the solution? *Leaders and managers should be equipped as change advocates to reinforce the purpose of the new process and its effective implementation. They should be prepared to provide reinforcement to team members when they are performing as expected and guidance for those who are not.* ❑ How will the organization promote learner autonomy? *This new approach to sales is putting more discretionary control directly into the hands of our sales team to manage their client relationships as compared with our current state. There will still be guidelines, but the process is one where the individual can control more about their deals than they do today.* **Additional Questions You Deem Relevant**

Intrinsic Enablers Debrief of Scenario 1

Given the answers and data collected, do you have any potential additional questions?

Intrinsic enablers are intended to leverage why learners personally care about the learning, and then find ways to infuse those enablers into the learning design itself. In this scenario, a few potential issues stand out.

► Lack of Personal Relevance

Stakeholders shared that their salespeople would see the obvious, innate value in the solution because it should lead to better business results. While this outcome may be true, it is not placing enough focus on individual benefits and is overly focused on what is good for the company. There should be increased messaging to trigger the learners' intrinsic motivation, making them want to learn the new approach.

► Unclear How Solution Will Facilitate Learners' Feelings of Competence

Feeling an increased sense of competence or mastery of a skill is a strong example of intrinsic motivation. The current responses from the stakeholder are focused on what they want to accomplish (relational selling), but they do not speak to how the new sales approach will help salespeople become more competent.

Additionally, as you reflect on earlier stakeholder responses in the Capacity and Layering domains for Scenario 1, the stakeholders seem to have limited appreciation for the practice and feedback necessary to master new behaviors required for relational selling.

What other questions would you ask to have enough information to begin designing a solution? We'll look at more with Scenario 1 in the next domain chapter, on Coherence, but for now, let's move to Intrinsic enablers considerations around a new hybrid model of work.

Scenario 2 (Priority-Driven)

Change management: Hybrid work model. As a reminder, here is some high-level background for this scenario:

Scenario 2: Company Details

Organization Type: National consumer products company

Employees: 60,000 nationally across the US

Footprint: Offices in New York, Atlanta, Dallas, Salt Lake, Los Angeles, and other facilities spread regionally

Stakeholders:
- Chief operations officer
- Chief HR officer
- Chief information officer
- Business unit leads

The Ask: Your organization is looking to enable hybrid ways of working following recent office closures due to the COVID-19 pandemic, as well as achieve long-term goals of enabling future-focused strategies of the workforce. As a result, training and change management is needed on new systems, processes, and behaviors among employees, as well as on how to interact with clients.

Speaking with your stakeholders, you can direct your questions using the CLICS Tool Core Questions in the table (or download the interactive PDF from the book website and add your own questions based on a real situation you currently face).

Stakeholder Responses on Intrinsic Enablers

In the next table, review the answers our stakeholders have provided.

Scenario 2: Learner-Relevant Considerations

Domains and Science	Learner-Relevant Considerations
Intrinsic enablers **Science:** • Intrinsic vs. extrinsic motivation • Relatedness • Competence • Autonomy • Self-concordance	**Why Will the Learner Care?** *Solution addresses meaning and relevance felt by learners* **Core Questions** ❑ How will the solution be relevant to learners? *Ideally the solution will give them more freedom to work from where they want, so hopefully they'll very much see the relevance. Without having to commute, even if only part time, that should give them even more time to focus on work and being productive.* ❑ How might the solution feel rewarding? *The opportunity to have more flexibility should be perceived as the extension of our trust in each other.* ❑ What level of autonomy will the solution support? *Learners should feel a significant increase in autonomy.* **Additional Questions You Deem Relevant**

Scenario 2: Workplace-Relevant Considerations

Domains and Science	👥 Workplace-Relevant Considerations
 Intrinsic enablers	**How Are Intrinsic Enablers Promoted?** *Solution incorporates environmental prompts that activate learners' intrinsic motivation* **Core Questions** ❑ How will the solution align to the organization's purpose? *It will increase worker productivity and hopefully engagement, as well as give the organization a stable set of conditions from which to plan corporate infrastructure, like real estate and technology investments.* ❑ How will leaders and managers reinforce the solution? *We will cascade this from the top and set the expectation that local managers will adopt this new flexibility in our approach to work.* ❑ How will the organization promote learner autonomy? *The goal is to set up the system in a way that individuals will be able to determine and forecast their work location and report it for others to know, based on the tasks they have at hand. If they need to be present for a meeting, they will. If they can work remotely, they will. It comes down to sharing that information with others.* **Additional Questions You Deem Relevant**

Intrinsic Enablers Debrief of Scenario 2

Given the answers and data collected, do you have any potential additional questions?

Remember that Intrinsic enablers tap into personal motivations and focus on why the individual should invest their time and energy to learn. The analysis goal is to understand how to best relate to the learner by increasing feelings such as competence, autonomy, or a sense of purpose. In this hybrid work scenario, there are two issues that need further exploration based on their responses.

► Individual Intrinsic Motivation Not Clearly Addressed

In this scenario, the stakeholders clearly have a vested interest in greater productivity, but there is no clear message about how the organization has taken employee intrinsic motivation into account with this new approach. It is unclear whether employees had a voice in shaping the new operational processes and policies necessary for hybrid work. That lack of input could backfire and be demotivating to those impacted.

► Unclear Alignment to Leadership Messaging

A second and even larger gap in the response is around manager preparedness to support and reinforce these changes. Being simply told that something is expected does not lead to a sense of autonomy or competence; in fact, it negatively impacts employees' intrinsic motivation to support the required behavior changes.

Assuming there are new behavioral norms, managers will need formal support and preparation to lead effectively in this new work environment. The value proposition needs to be more than "We're giving you greater flexibility, so we expect greater productivity."

In addition to clear messaging, the workplace environment must enable hybrid work or individuals will not feel the corresponding intrinsic motivation needed to drive lasting learning.

What other questions would you ask to have enough information to begin designing a solution? We'll look more into Scenario 2 in the next domain chapter, on Coherence, but for now, let's move to Intrinsic enablers considerations in Scenario 3.

Scenario 3 (Competency- or Role-Based)

Leadership development: Inclusivity. As a reminder, here is some high-level background for this scenario:

Scenario 3: Company Details

Organization Type: Global financial services

Employees: 100,000 globally

Footprint: Offices in North America; South America; Europe, Middle East, and Africa (EMEA)

Stakeholders: • Chief executive officer
  • Chief talent officer
  • Chief diversity officer (newly hired)
  • Board of directors

The Ask: Your organization is looking to support and empower broadscale updates to its corporate values in support of current DEI realities. The objective, and hope, of your stakeholders is to help the organization to attract and retain the top talent in the world around financial services. This includes the recent hiring of a chief diversity officer, who will be leading the delivery of this mandate from the CEO and board of directors.

Speaking with your stakeholders, you can direct your questions using the CLICS Tool Core Questions in the table (or download the interactive PDF from the book website and add your own questions based on a real situation you currently face).

Stakeholder Responses on Intrinsic Enablers

In the table, review the answers our stakeholders have provided.

Scenario 3: Learner-Relevant Considerations

Domains and Science	Learner-Relevant Considerations
Intrinsic enablers **Science:** • Intrinsic vs. extrinsic motivation • Relatedness • Competence • Autonomy • Self-concordance	**Why Will the Learner Care?** *Solution addresses meaning and relevance felt by learners* **Core Questions** ❑ How will the solution be relevant to learners? *The values of the company are changing and will be very relevant because our values are a very visible signal of who we are to our employees, our clients, and our stakeholders. When someone agrees to work here, they are by extension agreeing that their personal values align with ours and they are willing to support the company values.* ❑ How might the solution feel rewarding? *The shifts occurring will help us all feel more included, which we hope will result in greater success for both the organization and the individual, so that should be very rewarding. Inclusion is a very important business driver.* ❑ What level of autonomy will the solution support? *The solution should be very empowering because it overtly states and supports cultural values of diversity, equity, and inclusion, which are about ensuring every person will be heard.* **Additional Questions You Deem Relevant**

Scenario 3: Workplace-Relevant Considerations

Domains and Science	👥 Workplace-Relevant Considerations
Intrinsic enablers	**How Are Intrinsic Enablers Promoted?** *Solution incorporates environmental prompts that activate learners' intrinsic motivation* **Core Questions** ❑ How will the solution align to the organization's purpose? *The solution is very aligned with our purpose and goals, which is the reason the values are being added. We are demonstrating our commitment by hiring our new chief diversity officer and evolving the values to support those ideals in service of our purpose and goals.* ❑ How will leaders and managers reinforce the solution? *Leaders and managers will go through readiness sessions to bring them up to speed on new values, and at that time they'll be informed of expectations that they support the values. They should remind their colleagues of them in team meetings whenever possible.* ❑ How will the organization promote learner autonomy? *The new values set an expectation of greater inclusivity in our interactions with one another. This will give people the freedom to speak up and have a voice, which they say they want.* **Additional Questions You Deem Relevant**

Intrinsic Enablers Debrief of Scenario 3

Given the answers and data collected, do you have any potential additional questions?

In Scenario 3, two immediate opportunities to dig deeper stand out.

► Unclear Relatedness: Current Employee Inclusion Sentiment Not Covered

The request itself appears to be a reaction to external drivers. There is no mention of the current state of employee sentiment regarding inclusion among employees in the organization. While external data and indicators are critical, they should not be taken without the context of internal realities. The value proposition for the learners cannot be articulated without knowing how those same learners feel about the topic at hand. Clarity about the problem to be solved includes input from employees, or else they run the risk of not adopting their new values.

Here are some questions you might consider asking the stakeholder to get more of the necessary insight to inform a potential design:

- What kind of data does the organization have about how included employees feel today?
- What are the most essential behaviors that leaders need to demonstrate?
- What inclusion perspectives can be gleaned from exit interviews?

► Leader Modeling of Desired Behaviors Unclear and Preparation Ill-Defined

There was no discussion regarding the role of leaders in modeling the desired behaviors. There is no information shared in the responses about the preparation learners will receive to support the change in values. Additional questions might include:

- In engagement surveys, what behaviors are frequently cited for leaders who score highest on inclusivity?
- How has inclusivity been adapted for their major regions?
- What developmental opportunities have been provided to leaders to help them understand inclusivity?

We'll revisit Scenario 3 in chapter 6, on the Coherence domain. Next, let's review some key takeaways from the Intrinsic enablers domain when using CLICS to analyze your stakeholders' requests.

 Key Takeaways: Intrinsic Enablers

- Intrinsic enablers: the conditions required to enhance intrinsic motivation, to generate personal relevance and foster lasting learning
- Relevant science concepts
  - Intrinsic versus extrinsic motivation
  - Relatedness
  - Competence
  - Autonomy
- Analysis in action
  - Define the most important intrinsic motivators for the learners
  - Identify rewards and enablers that align with those intrinsic motivations
  - Explore how much autonomy the learners will have

CHAPTER 6
Applying Coherence

If you were asked, "What is your favorite movie?" how would you respond? When you think about your favorite movie, you probably can describe all the intricate details related to the plot, name specific characters, and even vividly imagine how they looked and sounded. Why are we so good at recalling details about our favorite movie, but we can't remember what we learned the other day in a workshop?

Minus the memorable visual scenes and melodic music, your favorite movie was easy to remember because it told a good story. Stories have the power to move you, captivate you, even inspire you. A good story constructs information in a meaningful and engaging way, whereas a bad story presents information in a disjointed and unmemorable way.

A good story has something scientists call coherence. Coherence is the cognitive ease with which information fits together and amplifies related ideas. Think of how puzzle pieces fit together—all the pieces are amplified by one another smoothly fitting together. In a coherent story, each part fits within the whole, so we have an easier time remembering an entire network of information versus individual pieces.

How to Leverage CLICS
In this chapter, we are focusing on the domain of Coherence (Figure 6-1).

Figure 6-1. Coherence Domain of CLICS

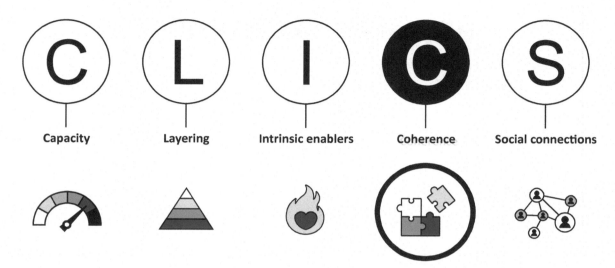

In today's complex and fast-moving organizations, it's not surprising that many decisions are made in silos, resulting in all the operational pieces not fitting together smoothly. When this happens, the effect is referred to as decoherence—when our brains receive conflicting information and overly invest time in trying to make sense of the fragments and misalignment.

What are some common signs of decoherence?

Learner-Relevant
- Inability to access training
- Learning programs that are poorly sequenced
- Conflicting curricula
- Inaccurate assumptions about learners' skills, knowledge, and motivations
- Too many work priorities within limited time
- Misaligned rewards and metrics
- Insufficient time for reinforcement (coaching, shadowing, or feedback)

Figure 6-2. Coherence Domain of CLICS Tool

Domains and Science	(⊙) Learner-Relevant Considerations	(♟) Workplace-Relevant Considerations
Coherence **Science:** • Associated network • Decoherent systems • Fluency	**How Big Is the Change?** *Solution associates new concepts with prior knowledge to promote adoption* **Core Questions** ❑ How does the solution fit with existing skills and knowledge? ❑ What context will help learners relate to the solution? ❑ How easy will the solution be for learners to understand? **Additional Questions You Deem Relevant**	**How Different Is the Desired State?** *Solution fits with, and is reinforced by, the workplace environment* **Core Questions** ❑ What leadership support is necessary to enable the change? ❑ What is different about the proposed change? ❑ What key elements in the workplace should change to support success? **Additional Questions You Deem Relevant**

Learner-Relevant Core Questions

To perform the analysis for the Coherence domain, we begin with three core questions about the learner:

1. **How does the solution fit with existing skills and knowledge?**

   Identifies the associations between the solution and what the learner already knows or can do.

2. **What context will help learners relate to the solution?**

   Identifies the explicit relevance of the solution to the learner.

3. **How easy will the solution be for learners to understand?**

   Identifies how much effort a learner must expend to grasp and apply the solution.

Workplace-Relevant Core Questions

To understand the environment that surrounds the learners, there are three core questions about the workplace itself:

1. **What leadership support is necessary to enable the change?**

   Identifies what actions are required to reinforce the relevance and importance of the intended solution.

2. **What is different about the proposed change?**

   Identifies potential gaps and the degree of effort and resources required to close them.

3. **What key elements in the workplace should change to support success?**

   Prioritizes elements of the environment that should change to reinforce the solution.

In addition, you can ask specific questions tailored to your situation, as the core questions are intended to capture the essential details necessary to design a solution that is aligned with stakeholder requirements.

Scenario 1 (Situational)

Improve business results: Revenue generation. As a reminder, here is some high-level background for this scenario:

Scenario 1: Company Details

Organization Type: Global products and services company

Employees: 25,000 worldwide

Footprint: Offices in North America; South America; Asia; and Europe, the Middle East, and Africa (EMEA)

Stakeholders:
- Chief revenue officer
- VP of sales
- Product marketing business unit lead

The Ask: Your organization's sales figures are not meeting projections, so the three stakeholders ask you to design and deploy training on some revised approaches to selling (such as moving from transactional-based selling to relational-based selling) and some new sales software to better manage the process.

Speaking with your stakeholders, you can direct your questions using the CLICS Tool Core Questions in the table (or download the interactive PDF from the book website and add your own questions based on a real situation you currently face).

Stakeholder Responses on Coherence

In the table, review the answers our stakeholders have provided.

Scenario 1: Learner-Relevant Considerations

Domains and Science	Learner-Relevant Considerations
Coherence **Science:** • Associated network • Decoherent systems • Fluency	**How Big Is the Change?** *Solution associates new concepts with prior knowledge to promote adoption* **Core Questions** ☐ How does the solution fit with existing skills and knowledge? *The new material is still sales training, so for our experienced folks it will be a process change in the way they approach things, but sales is still sales. It's about developing relationships with our clients. For new folks, it means not having to unlearn any old habits.* ☐ What context will help learners relate to the solution? *We want to highlight that the new sales process focuses on relational selling as a means of getting to know one's customers better and ultimately being able to understand how to meet their needs. Then we can propose deals that are more likely to close.* ☐ How easy will the solution be for learners to understand? *Honestly, this should not be that big of a lift. We are changing the processes that the team follows, but sales is sales. They still have to communicate with clients, which we already train them how to do.* **Additional Questions You Deem Relevant**

Scenario 1: Workplace-Relevant Considerations

Domains and Science	Workplace-Relevant Considerations
Coherence	**How Different Is the Desired State?** *Solution fits with, and is reinforced by, the workplace environment* **Core Questions** ☐ What leadership support is necessary to enable the change? *We are developing announcements to be made at the end-of-year sales event and later in ongoing sales meetings. It's important for us to be clear about what is expected.* ☐ What is different about the proposed change? *We're leaning into this new sales approach so we can build bigger books of business and improve our forecasts. Our current process focuses too much on the deal at hand and doesn't provide sales the flexibility they need to make better long-term client decisions.* ☐ What key elements in the workplace should change to support success? *We'll update the relevant training courses and then market them heavily during our sales team events.* **Additional Questions You Deem Relevant**

Coherence Debrief of Scenario 1

Given the answers and data collected, do you have any potential additional questions?

When assessing the Coherence domain, the goal is to determine how the proposed solution will make sense to the learners, given their existing knowledge and current environment. Based on the stakeholder responses, two areas of opportunity for further questioning include the following:

▶ Missing Associations From Current Approach and Desired Future State

The current stakeholder responses provided no clear associations from the current state to future state. Phrases like "this should not be a big lift" and "sales is sales" suggest that the leadership may have underestimated the degree of proposed change. While these perspectives may be common from senior leaders, they do not take into account how the learners may view the upcoming changes.

Also, there will be relational behaviors to learn and practice that accompany the new sales processes. Greater insights about the skills gap between current and future states are a must-have part of the analysis.

▶ High Probability of Poor Fluency

Given the multiple statements from the stakeholders that this request is an "easy" lift, you would expect weak fluency as a challenge to overcome. Fluency is the ease with which concepts are grasped by learners. Highly coherent, well-organized, and visually accessible materials would be categorized as having strong fluency. This fluency then minimizes the amount of cognitive effort needed to process new information and build the associated networks necessary to learn.

The stakeholder responses for this domain's considerations are missing much of this detail. The result of those gaps would be a solution with low fluency and high decoherence. This would show up as confusion about new sales processes, causing learners to feel uncertain about expectations, which could then undermine their execution.

We'll cover more on Scenario 1 in chapter 7, where we look at the considerations around the Social connections domain. Before we go there, however, let's look at the considerations for Coherence in Scenario 2.

Scenario 2 (Priority-Driven)

Change management: Hybrid work model. As a reminder, here is some high-level background for this scenario:

Scenario 2: Company Details

Organization Type: National consumer products company

Employees: 60,000 nationally across the US

Footprint: Offices in New York, Atlanta, Dallas, Salt Lake, Los Angeles, and other facilities spread regionally

Stakeholders:
- Chief operations officer
- Chief HR officer
- Chief information officer
- Business unit leads

The Ask: Your organization is looking to enable hybrid ways of working following recent office closures due to the COVID-19 pandemic, as well as achieve long-term goals of enabling future-focused strategies of the workforce. As a result, training and change management is needed on new systems, processes, and behaviors among employees, as well as on how to interact with clients.

Speaking with your stakeholders, you can direct your questions using the CLICS Tool Core Questions in the table (or download the interactive PDF from the book website and add your own questions based on a real situation you currently face).

Stakeholder Responses on Coherence

In the table, review the answers our stakeholders have provided.

Scenario 2: Learner-Relevant Considerations

Domains and Science	Learner-Relevant Considerations
Coherence **Science:** • Associated network • Decoherent systems • Fluency	**How Big Is the Change?** *Solution associates new concepts with prior knowledge to promote adoption* **Core Questions** ❑ How does the solution fit with existing skills and knowledge? *We currently have the ability for some people to work remotely, so this should really be no more than just expanding the awareness of the necessary tools and processes to more folks.* ❑ What context will help learners relate to the solution? *The freedom and flexibility that this program puts in the employees' hands should be obvious.* ❑ How easy will the solution be for learners to understand? *There will certainly be a ramp-up time for folks who are new to the increased freedom from working in a remote location, but the challenges are likely more in operations, ensuring our systems and tools are in place to provide greater remote access. The behaviors should come easily.* **Additional Questions You Deem Relevant**

Scenario 2: Workplace-Relevant Considerations

Domains and Science	Workplace-Relevant Considerations
Coherence	**How Different Is the Desired State?** *Solution fits with, and is reinforced by, the workplace environment* **Core Questions** ❑ What leadership support is necessary to enable the change? *We think leaders will be excited about the forecasted productivity gains from adopting a hybrid approach, so it will be a matter of letting them know the timing around moving into this model. We do have good representation from various tiers of leadership throughout the business that were part of the committee that evaluated our pilot program and gauged the feasibility of our plan.* ❑ What is different about the proposed change? *It differs from current norms in that we're putting trust in our people to have more self-determination around where and how to get their jobs done successfully. There will be guidelines and processes to enable that new work style, but this is about giving more flexibility to the employee while creating greater manager/peer awareness.* ❑ What key elements in the workplace should change to support success? *We will definitely need increased technical support for remote IT access and issues. Additionally, we are shifting from dedicated desk assignments to a flexible hoteling model to support a hybrid workforce.* **Additional Questions You Deem Relevant**

Coherence Debrief of Scenario 2

Given the answers and data collected, do you have any potential additional questions?

In looking at the Scenario 2 stakeholder responses, there are a couple of areas where more information is required.

▶ Incomplete Audience Definition

The stakeholders defined the learner population for the solution in the Capacity domain as "everyone in the organization," which is extremely broad in scope. The response for the Coherence domain ("just expanding . . . processes to more folks") seems to underestimate the change, setting up a situation where there will be learning gaps.

Assuming everyone in the organization is indeed the target learner population for this solution, then clear subdivisions need to be identified so a successful change management initiative can be developed for a hybrid work model.

▶ Leadership Support Seems Lacking Under Current Plan

The stakeholder response that "we think leaders will be excited" does not reflect any effort to create leadership buy-in. Given that this is a global organization, there are missing considerations regarding country and cultural differences that affect hybrid work and success.

The move to this new work model inherently requires leader and manager support. If the expectations of people leaders are not aligned with the long-term goal, there would be decoherence between the learning solution and the reality of how leaders and managers behave back on the job.

What other questions would you ask to have enough information to begin designing the right solution? We'll look at more with Scenario 2 in the next domain chapter, on Social connections, but for now, let's move to Coherence considerations for Scenario 3.

Scenario 3 (Competency- or Role-Based)

Leadership development: Inclusivity. As a reminder, here is some high-level background for this scenario:

Scenario 3: Company Details

Organization Type: Global financial services

Employees: 100,000 globally

Footprint: Offices in North America; South America; Europe, Middle East, and Africa (EMEA)

Stakeholders: • Chief executive officer
- Chief talent officer
- Chief diversity officer (newly hired)
- Board of directors

The Ask: Your organization is looking to support and empower broadscale updates to its corporate values in support of current DEI realities. The objective, and hope, of your stakeholders is to help the organization to attract and retain the top talent in the world around financial services. This includes the recent hiring of a chief diversity officer, who will be leading the delivery of this mandate from the CEO and board of directors.

Speaking with your stakeholders, you can direct your questions using the CLICS Tool Core Questions in the table (or download the interactive PDF from the book website and add your own questions based on a real situation you currently face).

Stakeholder Responses on Coherence

In the table, review the answers our stakeholders have provided.

Scenario 3: Learner-Relevant Considerations

Domains and Science	Learner-Relevant Considerations
Coherence **Science:** • Associated network • Decoherent systems • Fluency	**How Big Is the Change?** *Solution associates new concepts with prior knowledge to promote adoption* **Core Questions** ❑ How does the solution fit with existing skills and knowledge? *We don't see this as a large gap of skills and knowledge between the current and future state. It's more about an overt demonstration of commitment with the addition of the chief diversity officer.* ❑ What context will help learners relate to the solution? *We plan to demonstrate the key data points that typically make more diverse organizations more successful.* ❑ How easy will the solution be for learners to understand? *The solution should be fairly easy for the learners to grasp and put into action. It's mostly about raising awareness and making sure they clearly understand expectations around how to live and exhibit the values day-to-day.* **Additional Questions You Deem Relevant**

Scenario 3: Workplace-Relevant Considerations

Domains and Science	Workplace-Relevant Considerations
Coherence	**How Different Is the Desired State?** *Solution fits with, and is reinforced by, the workplace environment* **Core Questions** ❑ What leadership support is necessary to enable the change? *Leadership is clearly demonstrating its commitment to this change with a top-down approach to the rollout in setting clear expectations. Additionally, the chief diversity officer will launch a number of initiatives in the coming months to underscore the organization's commitment to this path.* ❑ What is different about the proposed change? *At its core, the proposed change is not vastly different from current norms. It is intended to be a clear, public declaration of the importance of diversity, equity, and inclusion by including the language in our values we live every day.* ❑ What key elements in the workplace should change to support success? *We're launching the values, the associated education, as well as the new initiatives led by the chief diversity officer. There is no need to change much of anything else in the workplace—we're already doing a lot.* **Additional Questions You Deem Relevant**

Coherence Debrief of Scenario 3

Given the answers and data collected, do you have any potential additional questions?

To achieve the Coherence necessary to successfully enable new business values, the stakeholder responses around Scenario 3 require more detail as follows.

► Missing Associations From Current to Future State

Based on the stakeholder responses here and in previous domains of the CLICS Tool, there's no plan to connect the current and future states. Learners need to appreciate the reasoning behind the new values so they can formulate their own connections. Instead, they say, "At its core, the proposed change is not vastly different from current norms." While this may be true, the new values require clear behaviors that demonstrate how the values should show up in their day-to-day work.

Absent these associations, the likelihood of decoherence is high for those being told to behave in new ways, as they have no clear understanding of how to do that successfully. To compound that, if the learners don't understand how to behave appropriately to support the new values, then leaders will be challenged to coach or set expectations that enable the new behaviors.

► Missing Schemas for Necessary Behavior Shifts

Examples of possible scenarios where the new values could be demonstrated are not clear. The context for when and how new behaviors should be applied are missing. Also absent are expectations for how learners would "live" the new values on a daily basis. The stakeholders don't see the need for a significant behavioral shift. "We don't see this as a large gap of skills and knowledge between the current and future state. It's more about an overt demonstration of commitment."

This lays the groundwork for significant decoherence between the expected and actual behaviors on the part of learners. Without the business context, learners will be forced to make assumptions about how to behave in the future state.

We'll revisit Scenario 3 in chapter 7, on the Social connections domain. Next, let's review some key takeaways from the Coherence domain when using CLICS to analyze your stakeholders' requests.

 Key Takeaways: Coherence

- Coherence: the cognitive ease with which information fits together and amplifies related ideas
- Relevant science concepts
  - Associated networks
  - Fluency
  - Decoherent systems
- Analysis in action
  - Determine the complexity of change required
  - Understand the organizational context and related curricula in place
  - Investigate organizational readiness to align related tools and processes

CHAPTER 7

Applying Social Connections

In the popular Harry Potter book series, Harry and his friends had to learn a defensive spell to ward off evil or harmful spirits. The Patronus spell required a wizard to conjure their most fond and positive memory, which was powerful enough to fight off the dark force. For most people, that spell would involve fond and positive memories of other people. Because we are inherently social beings, connecting to and through others is not only the best way to enhance our learning, but also the most natural way.

Social connections refer to the interpersonal support structure (physical, emotional, and psychological) that enables learning to be most effective. Our brains are wired to make social connections, and our memory is significantly enhanced by the presence of emotion. Understanding how to embed connections with others as part of learning is an essential ingredient for not only recall but also on-the-job application with colleagues.

How to Leverage CLICS

This chapter will explore how social connections help promote learning. This fifth domain of CLICS considers the opportunities in our interactions with other people to reinforce individual learning, as well as the chances for reinforcement of learning from the environment (Figure 7-1).

Figure 7-1. Social Connections Domain of CLICS

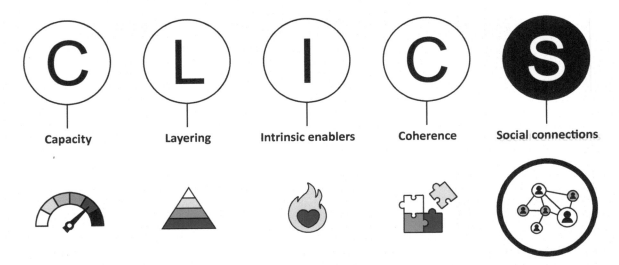

In our fast-moving digital world, it's tempting to focus on speed, scale, and the efficiency of reaching global audiences when conducting a needs analysis. Business leaders are often under pressure to quickly respond to market demands and competitive pressures. There once was a time when business leaders insisted on in-person learning and had to be convinced that a digital learning solution could work. Now it seems that the paradigm has shifted 180 degrees; leaders have to be convinced of the value of in-person learning, as the trade-offs and costs of being away from work can be significant. As a result of the global pandemic, colleagues now understand they can collaborate virtually, but the question still remains: What is the strength of social connections in a virtual environment?

There are clear examples of when relationships are central to business success:

- Building organizational trust
- Collaborating across the organization
- Establishing new relationships
- Repairing old relationships
- Onboarding new hires
- Fostering leadership alignment
- Developing cultural understanding
- Transforming operating models and roles
- Integrating mergers or acquisitions

- Driving rapid revenue growth
- Improving incident response capabilities
- Managing intense negotiations

No doubt attention to social connections is needed in these cases, but we would advocate that all learning is enhanced with social connections, as it's what our biology craves. Even if the content will be used independently, the use of reinforcement from others on the team can dramatically accelerate the application of new knowledge for their colleagues.

 Scientist Spotlight: Jamil Zaki, PhD
Professor, Stanford University; Author; Consultant

In 2016, there were 226 students enrolled in a challenging European engineering program. At the end of their first year, they would take an even more challenging exam, which fewer than half would pass. Who made it through? To predict the answer, you might look to students' GPAs, or their conscientiousness, and those factors matter. But so did their social lives. Researchers measured the network these students formed in their first year and found that social connections mattered enormously to academic success. Students who passed the exam made an average of 3.8 friends among their classmates; those who failed made just 2.6 friends. Why did this matter? Over the course of the year, friends became study buddies, and learning socially accelerated students' success (Stadtfeld et al. 2019).

People need social connection like fish need water. Friendships buoy our happiness and mental health. But they are just as important to learning and intellectual development. Social networks are also knowledge networks, and sharing information allows people to process it more deeply, consider different perspectives, and ultimately master material. Our culture often celebrates the lone genius, but advancing learning and knowledge is more often a team effort.

How to Assess Social Connections in the Workplace

When assessing the role social connections might play, it's helpful to imagine being the learner to determine the interpersonal interactions that would be beneficial. And broadly, there are two very important types of relationships a learner can have in organizations: mentors and peers.

Research Basis: Social Learning Theory

Rosa Parks once said, "Each person must live their life as a model for others." Role models are powerful influences whom we imitate and from whom we learn. We learn vicariously by watching how role models are rewarded versus punished. The most famous experiment done on social learning is known as the Bobo Doll study. In this study, children watched models who were aggressive with a plastic blow-up Bobo Doll and were respectively punished for their behavior or permitted to do it. Children who observed role models who were punished for their aggression behaved less aggressively toward the Bobo Doll compared with those who observed role models who were not punished for their aggression. Research, and our own intuitive experience, confirms that watching and learning from others directly shapes our own behaviors.

Defining the Role of Mentors and Peers

Mentors are invaluable for a type of instruction called scaffolding. Scaffolding is a technique where a mentor systematically provides support or guidance to assist in the mastery of skills. Mentors first anticipate potential challenges that learners will face and then create opportunities to guide learners through that challenge.

One way to connect this concept of scaffolding is to think about how to layer (think back to the chapter on Layering). What does the learner already know and what is the best way to layer new content so the learner can acquire new information? When in the learning process would be an optimal time to introduce the role of a mentor or to share insights from those who can role model the desired behaviors?

Peers, along with mentors, can also play a big role in affecting learning in the organization. Research shows that the relationship with peers is highly important and should not be excluded from the learning process. Peers can serve as "social vaccines" to help inoculate against harmful stereotypes and threats. For example, the presence of woman-identifying peers helps prevent gender stereotyping related to STEM subject competency, as they encourage younger women to study and remain in these fields (Dasgupta 2011). Such research shows that those around you greatly matter and can cultivate learning or even inadvertently cause people to leave a field or an industry entirely.

Research Basis: Social Norms

We are all familiar with peer pressure and often think of it as something teens go through. However, research shows us that peer pressure is strongly felt during adulthood, especially inside organizations. The presence of others greatly impacts the way one thinks and behaves, especially if we want to be accepted by them.

Solomon Asch conducted a string of experiments in the 1950s to determine how people are affected by the thoughts and behaviors of those around them. In one classic study, a group of participants viewed a diagram of lines that varied in length (Figure 7-2). The task was to identify the line (a, b, or c) that most closely resembled the prototype (x).

Figure 7-2. Asch's Conformity Study

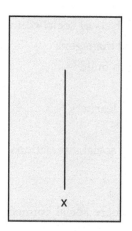 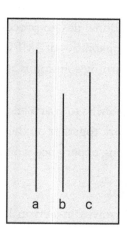

Line segments used in Asch's conformity study: Participants were asked to indicate which line segments (a, b, or c) most resembled the one on the left, line x (Asch 1951).

However, there was a trick in the experiment. Each group of participants had only one true, naive member, while the rest of the participants were planted by the researcher to manipulate the naive member. In this study, the confederates repeatedly and intentionally gave the wrong answer on each trial, pressuring the naive member to conform to the wrong answer.

Asch found that more than 75 percent of participants conformed to group pressure and provided the wrong answer. His study demonstrated the power of the group to influence an individual's judgment.

Expertise typically resides in some predictable roles, so it's important to inquire about both the readiness and the capacity of these roles to support workplace learning.

- **Subject matter experts (SMEs):** Individuals who have the greatest knowledge or skill in the organization. This could be someone in a formal role who oversees a process or a function, but it also could be a key influencer who has developed expertise in a given domain. These individuals serve as the primary source of information.
- **On-the-job peers:** Individuals who will work together and can reinforce and accelerate learning. There may be differences in experience levels that could be leveraged to help those with less experience develop faster. These individuals serve as an immediate source of support while actually conducting work.
- **Managers or team leads:** Individuals who set direction and provide guidance over time. Learning often requires a supportive environment where colleagues can experiment and potentially fail as they learn new skills or knowledge. These individuals serve as the main source of feedback, focusing on patterns of success, areas of improvement, and most importantly, progress.

In order to guide the instructional design process, the analysis of social connections should include an understanding of how to leverage the capabilities of SMEs, peers, and managers:

- Degree of expertise the learning solution is attempting to build
- Access to SMEs
- Willingness and ability of SMEs to coach and advise the learners
- Extent that groups will work together on the job
- How a synchronous learning experience would leverage social interactions

Fostering Social Connections

So much of formal education involves in-person learning, where social connections seem to flow rather easily. Inside organizational settings, however, there are different drivers of learning—timelines, budgets, regulatory compliance, market opportunities, health and safety issues; the list is quite long. With the rise of digital transformation and the mobility of the workforce, in-person learning increasingly has become a luxury.

Regardless, we know that interacting with others and experiencing those associated emotions amplifies attention, processing, and recall. Our challenge becomes understanding where the opportunities exist and how to leverage those for more effective learning.

Research Basis: Growth Mindset

Norms can encourage individuals to adopt a certain type of mindset geared to a culture in which it is safe to fail and struggle. Mindsets are lay theories people have about themselves and how the world works (Furnham 1988). For example, some people may believe intelligence is something innate and fixed, whereas others may believe that intelligence is something that can be developed and nurtured. Mindsets matter because they indicate deep, often unconscious assumptions that powerfully motivate people's thoughts, feelings, and behaviors. In other words, mindsets shape the meaning that people give to learning events, which then motivates specific responses in alignment with the held mindset.

Mindset often impacts how people apply what they've learned in these three ways. It:

- Determines what information you pay attention to in a given scenario
- Determines how your brain handles mistakes—either by activating learning and planning centers or by activating negative emotional responses
- Influences how you interpret and attribute your successes and failures and how you record those events in your long-term memory

People with a fixed mindset focus more—often unconsciously—on proving that they have a lot of ability and are good at what they do. Their experiences are dictated by a cyclical internal assessment of constant judgment, then using information as evidence either for or against evaluations, like whether they're successful or "good" at something. They see their performance as a test of their competence and self-worth (Dweck 2007).

On the other hand, those with a growth mindset believe that skills and abilities can be developed and that improving on your skills and abilities is the ultimate goal. With a growth mindset, the internal assessment is not one of judgment but one of constant scanning for opportunities to learn. These individuals are likely to adapt to change and find new ways to take constructive action.

Mindsets do all this, in large part, by changing the way your brain perceives any change that may affect you. A fixed mindset makes you more likely to view change as a threat, which leads to distress. You experience highly negative emotions and an inadequate or disorganized mobilization of physiological resources. Over time, this will lead you to feel less focused and less able to retain information. It may also make it increasingly difficult to learn new things or find adequate solutions to problems. Distress saps your energy and can undermine your mental and physical health in the long term.

Studies show that when you see change as a challenge, you experience eustress, the "good" stress. You experience an efficient and organized mobilization of physiological resources—your heart is more easily able to push blood through your circulatory system. Your ability to focus increases. You can think more deeply, encode new knowledge, and find new solutions.

> ### Case in Point: Kelly Palmer
> *Chief Learning Officer, Degreed; Author,* The Expertise Economy

Why are peer-to-peer networks so valuable?

KP: As my career has progressed, I've become increasingly committed to the power of peer networks. People value guidance and input from others with shared experiences, and they trust peers to provide the most relevant information. Peer content is typically focused, digestible, and tied directly to job performance. It's also an incredibly responsive mechanism to rapidly share information in the flow of work.

Why should learning organizations foster social connections?

KP: Traditional models of instructional design simply aren't fast enough to keep up with the volume and complexity of workplace demands. Content creator platforms should be an essential component of any learning technology architecture. In addition to peers sharing knowledge, organizations can develop skills in peer cohorts, guided but not controlled by experts. Today's workforce expects to be hyper-connected to one another.

What role does technology play in social connections?

KP: My career has always been closely associated with the tech sector, so I believe in the potential of technology when it's used wisely. Technology can close communication gaps, bring people together, foster relationships, and mitigate distance biases that lead to weaker decisions. It also can level the playing field, as it allows everyone to "see and be seen" in ways that promote fairness and inclusion.

How do social connections promote agility and innovation?

KP: There's nothing like a crisis to make us reassess our choices. One outcome of the COVID pandemic was the acceleration of change. We were forced to become suddenly agile, and we learned how to do things in six days that previously might have taken six months. Leaders were on full display real time, and the need for progress versus perfection ruled the day. Organizations became scrappy and learned how to quickly come together, innovate, and solve problems. We should carry those lessons forward as we continue to reimagine how work gets done.

With in-person learning, social connections happen almost organically. Through small group work, one-to-one feedback, and open dialogue, new relationships emerge and learning is enhanced. In addition, learners frequently spend time together outside of class and often form relationships that last long after class has ended.

While in-person learning is still an option, social platforms that expand collaboration, accelerate innovation, and remove physical distance have added new capabilities (and challenges) to organizational learning.

In a digital world, your analysis of how to foster social connections should explore the potential use of:

- Learning cohorts
- Small-team assignments
- One-to-one commitment partners
- Peer mentors or buddy systems
- Manager coaching
- Ongoing communities of interest
- Leaders as sponsors
- Alumni groups
- Post-program chat forums

Social Connections: An Analysis Application Guide

Using the three example scenarios introduced in previous chapters, you will now walk through the analysis dealing with the domain of Social connections. You can also visit the book website to download an editable version of the tool and apply it to your own or any situation.

The focus of the Social connections domain is that to truly maximize the potential for sustained and effective change, learners require opportunities to practice and apply the learning, but also to do so in an environment surrounded by social norms that reinforce the message and purpose of the change.

This occurs through identifying factors that impact them by asking "How will connections enhance learning?" (learner-relevant) and "How could connections be reinforced?" (workplace-relevant). Use these questions to identify how the change requires interactions with others to practice application of the change, as well as how the organization values and supports the required change by creating an environment of growth mindset necessary to support and reinforce the change.

The Social connections domain row from the CLICS Tool is extracted for reference as we walk through the three practical scenarios that follow (Figure 7-3).

Figure 7-3. Social Connections Domain of CLICS Tool

Domains and Science	👤 Learner-Relevant Considerations	👥 Workplace-Relevant Considerations
Social connections **Science:** • Social learning theory • Social norms • Growth mindset	**How Will Connections Enhance Learning?** *Solution promotes interactions with others to help embed new concepts* **Core Questions** ❑ With whom will learners practice? ❑ From whom will learners receive feedback? ❑ How will learners be able to observe role models in action? **Additional Questions You Deem Relevant**	**How Could Connections Be Reinforced?** *Solution uses tools and processes to drive interpersonal interactions that activate learning* **Core Questions** ❑ What tools will learners leverage to interact with one another? ❑ In what ways will leaders encourage collaboration to accelerate adoption? ❑ How will successes and failures be shared? **Additional Questions You Deem Relevant**

Learner-Relevant Core Questions

To perform the analysis for the Social connections domain, we ask three core questions:

1. **With whom will learners practice?**

   Helps to identify opportunities for practice and reinforcement of the solution's behaviors with others.

2. **From whom will learners receive feedback?**

   Helps to identify relevant sources of input regarding the learners' progress.

3. **How will learners be able to observe role models in action?**

   Helps to identify the right sources of support or correct guidance for learners to maximize their likelihood of learning the desired skills and behaviors.

Workplace-Relevant Core Questions

To consider what exists in the environment around prospective learners and how the learner-relevant considerations will impact the organization, we ask three core questions:

1. **What tools will learners leverage to interact with one another?**

   Identifies the resources learners will use to connect and collaborate.

2. **In what ways will leaders encourage collaboration to accelerate adoption?**

   Identifies the role leaders will play in fostering learning.

3. **How will successes and failures be shared?**

   Identifies how the culture promotes psychological safety so individuals can share with, and learn from, one another.

Beyond these core questions, you may ask additional questions pertinent to your given situation, but the sets of core questions are designed to capture minimum amounts of detail necessary to inform the design of an impactful solution based on stakeholder requirements.

Scenario 1 (Situational)

Improve business results: Revenue generation. As a reminder, here is some high-level background for this scenario:

Scenario 1: Company Details

Organization Type: Global products and services company

Employees: 25,000 worldwide

Footprint: Offices in North America; South America; Asia; and Europe, the Middle East, and Africa (EMEA)

Stakeholders:
- Chief revenue officer
- VP of sales
- Product marketing business unit lead

The Ask: Your organization's sales figures are not meeting projections, so the three stakeholders ask you to design and deploy training on some revised approaches to selling (such as moving from transactional-based selling to relational-based selling) and some new sales software to better manage the process.

Speaking with your stakeholders, you can direct your questions using the CLICS Tool Core Questions in the table (or download the interactive PDF from the book website and add your own questions based on a real situation you currently face).

Stakeholder Responses on Social Connections

In the table, review the answers our stakeholders have provided.

Scenario 1: Learner-Relevant Considerations

Domains and Science	👤 Learner-Relevant Considerations
Social connections **Science:** • Social learning theory • Social norms • Growth mindset	**How Will Connections Enhance Learning?** *Solution promotes interactions with others to help embed new concepts* **Core Questions** ❑ With whom will learners practice the solution? *Aside from the classes we want to run at the annual sales meeting and refresher sessions at the quarterly town hall, we see the salespeople practicing the relational behaviors on the job in their interactions with clients.* ❑ From whom will learners receive feedback? *The feedback will be in their results. If they get it, then their numbers will go up. If they don't get it, then their results will reflect that. From there, we'll figure out how to get them up to speed or not.* ❑ How will learners be able to observe role models in action? *We plan to share ongoing stories of success at the sales meetings and identify the folks who are getting it right. We'll make sure those individuals speak about what they do that works in those meetings.* **Additional Questions You Deem Relevant**

Scenario 1: Workplace-Relevant Considerations

Domains and Science	👥 Workplace-Relevant Considerations
Social connections	**How Could Connections Be Reinforced?** *Solution uses tools and processes to drive interpersonal interactions that activate learning* **Core Questions** ❑ What tools will learners leverage to interact with one another? *We see the classes as in-person training, and they'll get to do some run-throughs of the new approach to practice the new process. Also, we are expecting the team to document everything they're doing with clients in our CRM tool, so we could potentially make that visible to other salespeople.* ❑ In what ways will leaders encourage collaboration to accelerate adoption? *We plan to set team sales goals as well as individual goals. We hope this will cause folks to help each other out.* ❑ How will successes and failures be shared? *On our sales leader boards. Our top performers will be rewarded, and the ones who aren't succeeding will see themselves at the bottom of the board, which should motivate them to do more.* **Additional Questions You Deem Relevant**

Social Connections Debrief of Scenario 1

Given the answers and data collected, do you have any potential additional questions?

As we consider the Scenario 1 stakeholders' responses, there are two areas that stand out as needing more detail.

▶ Spacing for Practice Not Planned

So far, the plan is to dedicate a couple of days to learning at the upcoming sales meeting. The absence of other purposeful practice suggests that the stakeholders do not see the need for practice including spacing and repetition. The sales meeting can serve as an effective immersive environment for the sales team to build awareness of the new behaviors. Unfortunately, a single exposure to the concepts does not account for how most people effectively process new information and adopt new behaviors.

▶ Operating With a Fixed Mindset

The lack of a safe space to practice, receive feedback, and observe role-model behaviors should be discussed further. When stakeholders focus on business outcomes without a balanced concern for building skills and proficiency, this signals their culture might be oriented toward a fixed mindset. To foster individual growth and development, there should be a greater focus on progressive improvement over time. This requires an opportunity to practice, to fail, to reflect, to try again, and ultimately to improve.

Before we can build the right solution for Scenario 1, we should definitely ask more questions to get the details to carry forward into the design of the solution itself. Let's move next into the Social connections considerations for Scenario 2.

Scenario 2 (Priority-Driven)

Change management: Hybrid work model. As a reminder, here is some high-level background for this scenario:

Scenario 2: Company Details

Organization Type: National consumer products company

Employees: 60,000 nationally across the US

Footprint: Offices in New York, Atlanta, Dallas, Salt Lake, Los Angeles, and other facilities spread regionally

Stakeholders:
- Chief operations officer
- Chief HR officer
- Chief information officer
- Business unit leads

The Ask: Your organization is looking to enable hybrid ways of working following recent office closures due to the COVID-19 pandemic, as well as achieve long-term goals of enabling future-focused strategies of the workforce. As a result, training and change management is needed on new systems, processes, and behaviors among employees, as well as on how to interact with clients.

Speaking with your stakeholders, you can direct your questions using the CLICS Tool Core Questions in the table (or download the interactive PDF from the book website and add your own questions based on a real situation you currently face).

Stakeholder Responses on Social Connections

In the table, review the answers our stakeholders have provided.

Scenario 2: Learner-Relevant Considerations

Domains and Science	Learner-Relevant Considerations
Social connections **Science:** • Social learning theory • Social norms • Growth mindset	**How Will Connections Enhance Learning?** *Solution promotes interactions with others to help embed new concepts* **Core Questions** ❑ With whom will learners practice the solution? *They'll be practicing this with everyone as those employees that participate in hybrid work will still interact with those who aren't. We don't see this as needing a lot of practice as it's more about giving people the information, tools, and clearance from their managers to work this way.* ❑ From whom will learners receive feedback? *Because when working remotely, an even higher need for visibility and communication exists, learners will receive feedback on how the hybrid approach is working from their managers, but also from their peers and colleagues.* ❑ How will learners be able to observe role models in action? *Learners will have access to stories from individuals and teams who are successfully operating in a hybrid work environment.* **Additional Questions You Deem Relevant**

Scenario 2: Workplace-Relevant Considerations

Domains and Science	Workplace-Relevant Considerations
 Social connections	**How Could Connections Be Reinforced?** *Solution uses tools and processes to drive interpersonal interactions that activate learning* **Core Questions** ❏ What tools will learners leverage to interact with one another? *We plan to roll out broadly the Microsoft 365 applications to enable virtual communication and collaboration. This includes Teams, SharePoint, OneDrive, Whiteboard, and Planner. We will obviously need to ensure we have access to the relevant how-to training and documentation on these applications.* ❏ In what ways will leaders encourage collaboration to accelerate adoption? *Leaders will use team meetings to plan and launch hybrid work for their teams. We also intend for leaders to provide regular feedback to employees on how they manage the freedom of hybrid work relative to their overall productivity.* ❏ How will successes and failures be shared? *We see successes being shared via team meetings and failures shared via one-on-ones when leaders need to let employees know their productivity is not meeting expectations.* **Additional Questions You Deem Relevant**

Social Connections Debrief of Scenario 2

Given the answers and data collected, do you have any potential additional questions?

Similar to Scenario 1, the stakeholders in Scenario 2 appear to view this solution as raising technical awareness and not behavioral in nature. Successfully navigating sustained, hybrid work requires establishing social norms of expected behaviors and practices, both individually and within teams. To that end, here are a couple of areas of opportunity for further exploration.

▶ Leaders Ill-Prepared to Support Desired Social Norms

The stakeholders comment that managers will be providing feedback in team meetings and in one-on-ones, but there are not clear behavioral expectations, and there's no standard for "good" behaviors that a manager can use to provide feedback. Further definition in both of these dimensions is needed.

Stakeholders continue to assume that managers are prepared to provide feedback and are on board with the new program. This is evidenced by the stakeholder comment, "We don't see this as needing a lot of practice," signaling they see it as more of a tools and process implementation. The solution would need to include enablement for managers to lead, as well as for learners to perform, in the new hybrid work model.

► Missing Culture of Safety to Learn From Mistakes

The stakeholders' comment about not "needing a lot of practice" as well as how they discuss successes and failures are also issues. On the surface, this has the appearance of being respectful of their learners. However, from a social learning standpoint, more effective long-term learning happens in environments where learners have the opportunity to feel safe failing so they can learn from their mistakes and the mistakes of others.

Accepting and learning from low-risk failure first requires establishing a culture where learners feel it's safe to try new behaviors and know that they will not be penalized if they fail.

In large-scale change management initiatives, defining the social norms of how to work and lead effectively is critical. This situation deals explicitly with how the learners will work and interact with one another, which at its core is about social norms. The analysis for this scenario should include to whom the learner can turn for help, whom learners are encouraged to observe as roles models, and clarity about how one person's behavior will affect others in the enterprise.

Finally, let's look at the considerations around the Social connections of Scenario 3, which concerns the launch of revised company values with a focus on inclusion.

Scenario 3 (Competency- or Role-Based)

Leadership development: Inclusivity. As a reminder, here is some high-level background for this scenario:

Scenario 3: Company Details

Organization Type: Global financial services

Employees: 100,000 globally

Footprint: Offices in North America; South America; Europe, Middle East, and Africa (EMEA)

Stakeholders:
- Chief executive officer
- Chief talent officer
- Chief diversity officer (newly hired)
- Board of directors

The Ask: Your organization is looking to support and empower broadscale updates to its corporate values in support of current DEI realities. The objective, and hope, of your stakeholders is to help the organization to attract and retain the top talent in the world around financial services. This includes the recent hiring of a chief diversity officer, who will be leading the delivery of this mandate from the CEO and board of directors.

Speaking with your stakeholders, you can direct your questions using the CLICS Tool Core Questions in the table (or download the interactive PDF from the book website and add your own questions based on a real situation you currently face).

Stakeholder Responses on Social Connections

In the table, review the answers our stakeholders have provided.

Scenario 3: Learner-Relevant Considerations

Domains and Science	Learner-Relevant Considerations
Social connections **Science:** • Social learning theory • Social norms • Growth mindset	**How Will Connections Enhance Learning?** *Solution promotes interactions with others to help embed new concepts* **Core Questions** ❑ With whom will learners practice the solution? *The new values will be put into practice each day by everyone at the company as they interact with one another and our clients.* ❑ From whom will learners receive feedback? *Employees will receive feedback from their managers and their peers on how effectively they are living and demonstrating the new values.* ❑ How will learners be able to observe role models in action? *Employees will have access to success stories based on the new values via the company intranet as well as in team meetings, where leaders will share informally.* **Additional Questions You Deem Relevant**

Scenario 3: Workplace-Relevant Considerations

Domains and Science	👥 Workplace-Relevant Considerations
  Social connections	**How Could Connections Be Reinforced?** *Solution uses tools and processes to drive interpersonal interactions that activate learning* **Core Questions** ❑ What tools will learners leverage to interact with one another? *We will use virtual collaboration tools to build relevant communities of practice. Once deployed, they will give employees a place to discuss situations relevant to the values and how those values are demonstrated.* ❑ In what ways will leaders encourage collaboration to accelerate adoption? *Leaders will actively participate in group discussions with their team to ensure understanding and successful demonstration of the values by their staff.* ❑ How will successes and failures be shared? *Team and individual successes will be shared throughout the organization by our corporate communications group. We plan to announce our new values on our external website as we want to be transparent with potential employees and clients about who we really are. As for failures, we will work to identify those internally and seek to correct the situation as quickly as possible.* **Additional Questions You Deem Relevant**

Social Connections Debrief of Scenario 3

Given the answers and data collected, do you have any potential additional questions?

This scenario deals with new company values of inclusion, and how important it is to have a clear understanding of the desired behaviors that will demonstrate successfully achieving and living those values. With social connections and the need for clearly defined behaviors to be described to learners in mind, there are two areas of opportunity for more consideration.

► Missing Mechanism to Practice Behaviors

The stakeholder responses for both the learner and workplace considerations do not provide sufficient detail about how the learners will actually practice the behaviors that align to the values. This is likely because the behaviors haven't been identified yet. Taking the stakeholder responses at face value, it would seem their desire is to launch the new values and have learners practice those values exclusively in their day-to-day performance of assigned job responsibilities.

For effective learning of what the new values mean in practice, the participants need the space to understand how the values translate into behaviors, and then have an opportunity to put those behaviors into practice with their peers. With access to role models and a safe space for feedback, individuals will be able to learn from mistakes, not just their successes. The opportunity to practice with peers is an area to define more with the stakeholders, and it leads to the next area of opportunity below.

☛ No Allowance for Mistakes and Growth

The stated plan from the stakeholders in this domain focuses exclusively on successes, sharing them openly via multiple channels. Conversely, mistakes and failures would appear to be something to handle discreetly and quietly. A growth mindset and continuous learning culture would focus on improvement, not perfection. For learners, understanding how to improve requires being able to meaningfully look at not just the times they got it right, but also when they didn't. In terms of social connections, it is equally important mistakes are shared publicly and are communicated as lessons learned so others can see what doesn't work just as readily as they can see what does.

It is important in this situation to go back and ask the stakeholders for more information about how the solution will support their desired objectives, taking these principles of effective social connections into account.

Before going on to chapter 8, where we look at the CLICS Tool in total, let's review some key takeaways from the Social connections domain when using CLICS to analyze your stakeholders' requests.

 Key Takeaways: Social Connections

- Social connections: the interpersonal support structure (physical, emotional, and psychological) necessary for optimal learning
- Relevant science concepts
  - Social learning theory
  - Social norms
  - Growth mindset
- Analysis in action
  - Identify who will provide feedback and reinforcement
  - Discuss how successes and failures will be shared among colleagues
  - Determine how leaders will model support and encourage collaboration

CHAPTER 8
The CLICS Tool in Total

In prior chapters for the individual CLICS domains, we reviewed some typical pitfalls stakeholders encounter when talking about learning solutions. The key to successfully obtaining the necessary information from stakeholders is a matter of asking good questions.

In this chapter, we consider the CLICS Tool as a whole with some senior stakeholders who are a little more thoughtful about the factors for effective learning outcomes. This time around, we revisit Scenario 1 to see if the stakeholders can focus a bit more on what is required to support their colleagues.

The CLICS Tool and Your Needs Analysis

Figure 8-1 provides a few reminders about the CLICS tool.

Figure 8-1. CLICS Framework: Learning Analysis Question Tool

Domains and Science	👤 Learner-Relevant Considerations	🐝 Workplace-Relevant Considerations
Capacity Science: • Finite working memory • Consequences of cognitive overload • Methods to enhance capacity	**How Much Is Sufficient?** *Solution balances how much information is essential versus how much learners can process, recall, and apply* **Core Questions** ❑ What outcomes are required to achieve success? ❑ Who are the essential learners to inform the learning requirements? ❑ How significant or complex is the necessary behavior change? **Additional Questions You Deem Relevant**	**What Will Compete or Distract?** *Solution considers competing initiatives and distractors to maximize learners' attention* **Core Questions** ❑ What other initiatives are currently planned that impact the learners? ❑ How will the organization prioritize the solution over competing demands? ❑ How could implementation be segmented to optimize learning? **Additional Questions You Deem Relevant**
Layering Science: • Schema acquisition • Spacing • Repetition	**What Structure Makes Sense?** *Solution integrates sequence, spacing, and frequency of critical concepts* **Core Questions** ❑ How will the new solution build on existing capabilities? ❑ What remedial support or incremental skills and knowledge are necessary? ❑ How much time will learners have to learn new concepts? **Additional Questions You Deem Relevant**	**How Does It Build on What Exists?** *Solution has purposeful connections to the workplace environment* **Core Questions** ❑ What related learning elements already exist? ❑ How capable are managers of reinforcing through feedback? ❑ What messaging will reinforce what has been learned? **Additional Questions You Deem Relevant**
Intrinsic enablers Science: • Intrinsic vs. extrinsic motivation • Relatedness • Competence • Autonomy • Self-concordance	**Why Will the Learner Care?** *Solution addresses meaning and relevance felt by learners* **Core Questions** ❑ How will the solution be relevant to learners? ❑ How might the solution feel rewarding? ❑ What level of autonomy will the solution support? **Additional Questions You Deem Relevant**	**How Are Intrinsic Enablers Promoted?** *Solution incorporates environmental prompts that activate learners' intrinsic motivation* **Core Questions** ❑ How will the solution align to the organization's purpose? ❑ How will leaders and managers reinforce the solution? ❑ How will the organization promote learner autonomy? **Additional Questions You Deem Relevant**
Coherence Science: • Associated network • Decoherent systems • Fluency	**How Big Is the Change?** *Solution associates new concepts with prior knowledge to promote adoption* **Core Questions** ❑ How does the solution fit with existing skills and knowledge? ❑ What context will help learners relate to the solution? ❑ How easy will the solution be for learners to understand? **Additional Questions You Deem Relevant**	**How Different Is the Desired State?** *Solution fits with, and is reinforced by, the workplace environment* **Core Questions** ❑ What leadership support is necessary to enable the change? ❑ What is different about the proposed change? ❑ What key elements in the workplace should change to support success? **Additional Questions You Deem Relevant**
Social connections Science: • Social learning theory • Social norms • Growth mindset	**How Will Connections Enhance Learning?** *Solution promotes interactions with others to help embed new concepts* **Core Questions** ❑ With whom will learners practice? ❑ From whom will learners receive feedback? ❑ How will learners be able to observe role models in action? **Additional Questions You Deem Relevant**	**How Could Connections Be Reinforced?** *Solution uses tools and processes to drive interpersonal interactions that activate learning* **Core Questions** ❑ What tools will learners leverage to interact with one another? ❑ In what ways will leaders encourage collaboration to accelerate adoption? ❑ How will successes and failures be shared? **Additional Questions You Deem Relevant**

Keep in mind the **dual** considerations of all five domains for both the learner and the workplace ecosystem the solution will be deployed into. Each will influence your outcomes.

For each domain, remember that while the tool has starter questions, you can ask more and different questions. The point is getting enough detail to create an effective solution.

CLICS is not necessarily procedural, and you may complete it over the course of multiple discussions with different stakeholders, but Capacity will likely come first because this domain is where you'll identify the required audience.

While all five CLICS domains are important, the Capacity and Coherence domains are typically the most critical to get across with senior stakeholders. You can get details around the other three from members of their team.

Scenario 1 (Situational) Revisited

Improve business results: Revenue generation. In chapter 1, one of three learning scenarios was based on a stakeholder request for new sales training. The organization's main goal was to improve business performance through the generation of increased revenue. In that scenario, as covered in the domain chapters, you saw some of the typical pitfalls when stakeholders (and their learning partners) don't consider the domains of CLICS.

Here, we'll revisit that scenario to look at stakeholder responses that are more aligned with the CLICS framework, and provide a stronger analysis of the requirements for the requested sales training solution.

As a reminder, here is some high-level background for this scenario:

Scenario 1: Company Details

Organization Type: Global products and services company

Employees: 25,000 worldwide

Footprint: Offices in North America; South America; Asia; and Europe, the Middle East, and Africa (EMEA)

Stakeholders:
- Chief revenue officer
- VP of sales
- Product marketing business unit lead

The Ask: Your organization's sales figures are not meeting projections, so the three stakeholders ask you to design and deploy training on some revised approaches to selling (such as moving from transactional-based selling to relational-based selling) and some new sales software to better manage the process.

Speaking with your stakeholders, you can direct your questions using the CLICS Tool Core Questions in the table (or download the interactive PDF from the book website and add your own questions based on a real situation you currently face).

Stakeholder Responses on Capacity

Review the answers your stakeholders have provided in the tables.

Domains and Science	⊗ Learner-Relevant Considerations
Capacity **Science:** • Finite working memory • Consequences of capacity • Methods to improve memory	**How Much Is Sufficient?** *Solution balances how much information is essential versus how much learners can process, recall, and apply* **Core Questions** ❏ What are required outcomes to achieve success? *We are looking to evolve our existing sales skills while also putting in place a program that sets new joiners up for success. To generate more revenue and more meaningful client relationships, we are looking to upskill our team to deliver on relational, solution-based sales processes around qualification, selling, servicing, and relationship management. We have a number of objectives and key results (OKRs) linked to these areas that will help us identify and track status and success.* ❏ Who are the essential learners to inform the learning requirements? *The focus will be on updating elements of our overall sales curriculum to address areas impacted by the new behaviors, processes, and technologies required to support this new strategy and sales philosophy. This will mean upskilling existing employees as well as updating our program for new joiners. The audience for the sales curriculum includes:* *• Salespeople (6,000 people globally)* *• Client success managers (1,500 people globally)* *• Sales fulfillment (1,500 people in three main fulfillment centers)* ❏ How complex is the necessary behavior change? *There are some key nuances to this new approach that differ from our current state. Our sales curriculum includes four primary areas: core sales skills, products and markets, sales process, and customer experience.* *Except for products and markets, there will be elements of each area that change to reflect the newly desired behaviors, as well as updated technology and processes to support things along the way. This is a fairly significant lift, impacting multiple roles in a number of ways, and as such will require a well-designed approach to deliver an end-to-end solution that will help the entire function achieve our plan.*

Domains and Science	Workplace-Relevant Considerations
Capacity	**What Will Compete or Distract?** *Solution considers competing initiatives and distractors to maximize learners' attention* **Core Questions** ❑ What other initiatives are currently planned that impact the learners? *Currently we're coming up on the end of both the quarter and the fiscal year, so the sales function will be very focused on closing out existing pipeline deals and finding new ones. They also need to complete annual compliance training courses for the new fiscal year.* *When we get a final list of all impacted roles, we will also provide a calendar of operational events for each. This sales philosophy shift is a priority for us, and you will have the full support of the sponsorship team.* ❑ How will the organization prioritize the solution over competing demands? *The new sales approach, and all that it entails, is a key strategic differentiator for the company this year, and our executive team is prepared to adjust other commitments as needed. Depending on the solution plan and design, we're open to flexible delivery to reach the necessary staff this coming year.* ❑ How could implementation be segmented to optimize learning? *We want to deliver the new training to all salespeople at the year-end sales meeting next month. The current year results will be reviewed, and new product strategies and offerings will be launched. We can do quarterly refresh sessions next year as well if needed.*

Scenario 1 Revisited: Capacity Debrief

In reading the stakeholder responses this time, did you detect a different level of focus on learner needs and environmental awareness?

This time around, the stakeholders seem much more focused on clearly defining the audience. They recognize the complexities of ongoing business operations and the global nature of the rollout in their responses. The statement that there are clear OKRs is also reassuring, as there will be defined ways to measure success.

Stakeholder Responses on Layering

Review the answers your stakeholders have provided in the table.

Domains and Science	👤 Learner-Relevant Considerations
  Layering **Science:** • Schema acquisition • Spacing • Repetition	**What Structure Makes Sense?** *Solution integrates sequence, spacing, and frequency of critical concepts* **Core Questions** ❏ How will the new solution build on existing capabilities? *For existing employees, two elements of the solution we would like to include are a change map indicating what will shift within the current sales curriculum, and an assessment instrument to help measure current levels of skills for impacted roles. This should help provide a transition road map for existing employees.* ❏ What remedial support or incremental skills and knowledge are necessary? *Our hope is that some components of the updated curriculum will be self-paced, as this will enable individual employees to focus on aspects of the new process that is specific to them, as well as any areas that may need remediation.* ❏ How much time will learners have to learn new concepts? *Knowing that the audience will contain many roles in many different locations, we understand that there needs to be some flexibility regarding the sequence of components during delivery. We envision this training to be accompanied by a broader marketing plan to communicate the upcoming change as well as the localized change plans as they become available. Our hope is that we'll transition the organization into the new approach, technologies, and processes this year with a staggered rollout by target audience.*

Domains and Science	Workplace-Relevant Considerations
 Layering	**How Does It Build on What Exists?** *Solution has purposeful connections to the workplace environment* **Core Questions** ❏ What related learning elements already exist? *As mentioned, we see this solution as a series of updates to elements of the core sales skills, sales process, and customer experience aspects of our existing sales curriculum. Our thinking is we need to approach this as a planned remediation rollout for current sales employees. We also want to go live ASAP with the new version of the sales curriculum for anyone newly hired into sales.* ❏ How capable are managers of reinforcing through feedback? *We will continue to engage our frontline managers as champions, asking them to provide real-time feedback following client sales meetings. Additionally, people leaders for impacted roles within the function should be prioritized to go through available training elements first to prepare them to support their teams as they transition to the new sales process.* ❏ What messaging will reinforce what has been learned? *We have existing incentives and rewards built into our sales teams' compensation plans. We'll be amending incentives to align with the new processes and targets, and we'll share those as part of the rollout.*

Scenario 1 Revisited: Layering Debrief

In reading the stakeholder responses this time about Layering, did you detect a different level of focus on learner needs and environmental awareness?

There's recognition that different paths are necessary for existing employees and new hires. Also, defining pathways by role based on assessing current skills and knowledge shows that these stakeholders have thought things through.

It is helpful to see how the stakeholders have considered the new solution in comparison to the current sales curriculum and have made a clear distinction. They acknowledged that changes are needed, but can see how the new program needs to build on existing points of reference.

Stakeholder Responses on Intrinsic Enablers

Review the answers your stakeholders have provided in the table.

Domains and Science	👤 Learner-Relevant Considerations
Intrinsic enablers **Science:** • Intrinsic vs. extrinsic motivation • Relatedness • Competence • Autonomy • Self-concordance	**Why Will the Learner Care?** *Solution addresses meaning and relevance felt by the learners* **Core Questions** ❑ How should the solution be relevant to learners? *The new approach to sales is intended to help make them more productive, so that should make it very relevant. It will help them establish sound, long-lasting relationships with their clients, which will make better use of their time.* ❑ How might the solution feel rewarding? *The goal is to set the employees up for success by promoting a philosophy of relational selling over transactional selling. We want employees to develop feelings of confidence by understanding their clients' needs more fully and being able to serve them better in the long run. That's much more productive than dealing with cold lead after cold lead, just to get a one-time sale that likely won't repeat.* ❑ What level of autonomy will the solution support? *The relational sales approach and processes we are adopting are intended to help the salesperson connect regularly with their clients. A primary benefit to this approach is to demonstrate more trust in sales and give them control over the approach they take with their accounts, encouraging them to focus on their clients' needs.*

Domains and Science	👥 Workplace-Relevant Considerations
Intrinsic enablers	**How Are Intrinsic Enablers Promoted?** *Solution incorporates environmental prompts that activate learners' intrinsic motivation* **Core Questions** ❑ How will the solution align to the organization's purpose? *The new sales philosophy links our employees' success with the goal of building long-lasting relationships with our clients. We would like to see this connection emphasized in the training and change-supporting communications, as it signals we are being purposeful in how the new approach will enable both our employees and clients.* ❑ How will leaders and managers reinforce the solution? *Leaders and managers will be equipped as change advocates to reinforce the purpose of the new process and its effective implementation. They should be prepared to provide positive reinforcement to team members when they are performing as expected, and developmental support for those who are not.* ❑ How will the organization promote learner autonomy? *This new approach to sales is putting more control directly into the hands of our sales team to manage their client relationships as compared with our current state. While guidelines and processes will still exist, the new process emphasizes a more tailored approach between sales employees and their clients.*

Scenario 1 Revisited: Intrinsic Enablers Debrief

In reading the stakeholder responses this time about Intrinsic enablers, did you sense a different level of focus on learner needs and environmental awareness?

This version demonstrates that the stakeholders had a much clearer grasp of the individual learner need for autonomy and competence. Additionally, they recognized the significance of linking the organization's purpose to the goals of the individual to create a sense of shared purpose. They were also explicit about an existing expectation for leaders and managers to act as change advocates, reinforcing and supporting the new solution.

Stakeholder Responses on Coherence

Review the answers your stakeholders have provided in the table.

Domains and Science	🧑 Learner-Relevant Considerations
Coherence **Science:** • Associated networks • Schemas • Fluency	**How Big Is the Change?** *Solution associates new concepts with prior knowledge to promote adoption* **Core Questions** ❑ How does the solution fit with existing skills and knowledge? *Our products and services are effectively remaining the same, so the goal is to bridge from what is already known, adding ideas that are new. We will continue to stress our core sales philosophy, long-term relationships, and client service over short-term transactional gains. The technology and processes are being retooled to emphasize more client relationship management (CRM) than is in our current state. That will be a larger lift to be sure.* ❑ What context will help to demonstrate the solution's value? *We plan to share the research as well as our own internal analysis about the long-term value of our clients. We'll also highlight our ongoing successes, including how we will build on our existing sales methods and training. We plan to highlight that the new sales process is a means of getting to know customers better and ultimately proposing deals that are more likely to close. Additionally, by focusing on long-term relationships, we should be more efficient in managing existing relationships as opposed to the time-consuming effort of developing new clients with every transaction.* ❑ How easy will the solution be for learners to understand? *This is a pretty significant, complex shift for the company, compounded by our global nature and the need for unique paths by role and by location. We are hoping that moving into the solution in a purposeful way over an extended period will give our current staff time to process the changes effectively.*

Domains and Science	Workplace-Relevant Considerations
  Coherence	**How Different Is the Desired State?** *Solution fits with, and is reinforced by, the workplace environment* **Core Questions** ❑ What leadership support is necessary to enable the change? *We recognize the scope and complexity of this shift. The leadership team is totally on board to keep this moving. They are willing to communicate regularly and demonstrate their commitment with the investment of time and resources. We also have vocal support for the program from the CEO.* ❑ What is different about the proposed change? *We're leaning into this new sales approach so we can build bigger, more predictable books of business that will ultimately improve our forecasts. Our current process focuses too much on the deal at hand and doesn't provide sales the flexibility they need to make better long-term client decisions. While it will take time to build the relationships we're looking for, that effort won't have to be repeated with each new deal, but rather with each new client.* ❑ What key elements in the workplace should change to support success? *In addition to adjustments to the sales curriculum, we have developed an extensive change and marketing communications plan. We've also established a new role: a formal VP of client success to head up ongoing client relationship management. This role will be a peer to our VP of sales, and both will report to the chief revenue officer.*

Scenario 1 Revisited: Coherence Debrief

In reading the stakeholder responses this time related to Coherence, did you detect a different level of focus on learner needs and environmental awareness?

One source of relief was the outright recognition of the significant size and complexity of the change surrounding this initiative. There are multiple roles, platforms, and processes necessary to make the program successful, and that is compounded by a global workforce with unique needs by location. However, this set of senior stakeholders has also committed to the vocal and visible support required to make the solution a success. Also, they are planning to share relevant sales performance data that will demonstrate the value of long-term client relationships.

Stakeholder Responses on Social Connections

Review the answers your stakeholders have provided in the table.

Domains and Science	⊙ Learner-Relevant Considerations

Social connections

Science:
- Social learning theory
- Social norms
- Growth mindset

How Will Connections Enhance Learning?
Solution promotes interactions with others to help embed new concepts

Core Questions
❏ With whom will learners practice?
Aside from the classes we will offer at the annual sales meeting and the refresher sessions at the quarterly town hall, we see the learners practicing these new relational behaviors on the job with clients. They also can leverage their team meetings with colleagues and managers as dry runs prior to client meetings. We plan to formalize a debrief process following client meetings to share what went well, and what could go better, and socialize lessons learned with others.

❏ From whom will learners receive feedback?
The feedback will come from peers and colleagues in training sessions, sales team practice activities, and real client interactions. The goal is to grow, be better, and learn from one another. Our managers will need to learn the new processes so they can be effective coaches.

❏ How will learners be able to observe role models in action?
Learners will be able to observe role-modeling at each stage of the process, in the learning activities, in team practice sessions, and before and after client interactions. We have some very talented sales professionals in our organization, many of whom will adapt quickly and become role models for their peers.

Domains and Science	⧀ Workplace-Relevant Considerations

Social connections

How Could Connections Be Reinforced?
Solution uses tools and processes to drive interpersonal interactions that activate learning

Core Questions
❏ What tools will learners leverage to interact with one another?
We see the classes being delivered in person, where learners will role-play the new approach to practice what they've learned. We are expecting the team to document everything they're doing with clients in our CRM tool, so we could potentially make that visible to other salespeople. Additionally, we're looking at community-based online platforms to share best practices and lessons learned.

❏ In what ways will leaders encourage collaboration to accelerate adoption?
In addition to the team meetings, client pre- and post-interaction debriefs are critical. Leaders will coach practice sessions and lead discussions on what works and what doesn't. We believe having team sales goals in addition to individual goals will encourage people to work together.

❏ How will successes and failures be shared?
Successes and failures will be shared openly, on results dashboards visible to all, and in town halls and team meetings. The goal of this is to promote a culture where we learn from each other's successes (to repeat) and failures (to avoid). Our senior leaders will lead by example, including sharing their "miss of the month" in monthly meetings.

Scenario 1 Revisited: Social Connections Debrief

In reading the stakeholder responses related to social connections this time, did you detect a different level of focus on learner needs and environmental awareness?

The requested solution has significant behavioral and procedural elements that will require multiple roles working in new ways. This is a solution that absolutely will require social learning and connections to be successful. The stakeholder responses convey that they understand the importance of practice and feedback at multiple points of the solution (for example, in formal learning, in team meetings, and around client interactions). This willingness to embrace a growth mindset and create a culture of safety that actively seeks to not only share examples of what is right but also promote lessons learned to minimize mistakes being repeated will help with success.

Looking Ahead

If you successfully address the considerations of the CLICS framework when completing your needs analysis with stakeholders, you are much more likely to come away with the specific information and details you need to design and develop an effective solution. In chapter 9, we take a brief look at what this might look like when applying CLICS to the design and development of your learning solutions.

CHAPTER 9
CLICS in Design and Development

Because the overall goal of CLICS is to maximize sustained individual learning in an organizational context, the process of design and development is a natural extension of analysis. When initially examining the learning challenge during the needs analysis, the application of CLICS centers around clarifying the requirements of the request, while taking into account specific needs and characteristics of the target learner population and the environment in which they work.

The early stages of discussion are about defining the *what* of the solution—the scope and scale. The purpose of analysis is to press your stakeholders on what they are really looking to accomplish with their request and who is really necessary to achieving it. The intent is to zero in on those elements that are essential, not exhaustive—what is absolutely necessary to achieve the desired outcomes while accounting for what learners need to learn.

After defining an accurate scale of the desired solution, you are ready to apply the same considerations of CLICS to design a solution that achieves your stakeholder objectives while also serving the learner. Discovering how to close the gap between the reality of the stakeholder requirements and the needs of the learners is what makes CLICS a learner-centered framework grounded in design thinking.

The principles of CLICS hold true regardless of the particular instructional systems design (ISD) methodology your organization may use, such as:
- ADDIE
- Agile/Successive Approximation Model (SAM)
- ARCS
- ASSURE
- Owens-Kadakia Learning Cluster Design (OK-LCD)

The key is applying your understanding of the learner and their environment through the lens of your stakeholders' desired outcomes. In the next sections, we examine how the domains of CLICS—Capacity, Layering, Intrinsic enablers, Coherence, and Social connections—can influence and shape your solution design.

How to Integrate Capacity When Designing Solutions

The Capacity domain of CLICS focuses on the cognitive capacity and resources needed to meaningfully process information. When we are confronted with too much at one time, our brain's ability to process the input ceases because it is overloaded. Additionally, we do not tend to learn new information in a single encounter.

During the analysis phase, you likely landed on a certain volume of information that learners will need to process as part of the potential solution. The challenge in the next phase of solution development is to consider that body of information and how best to present it to the learners so it will set them up for success. A strong design will avoid overloading learners' cognitive capacity and maximize the likelihood that they will process and remember what you're asking them to learn.

To this end, try using these techniques when designing your solution:

- Chunking and spacing
- Mnemonic devices
- Operations calendar timing

Chunking and Spacing

Chunking and spacing techniques focus on how to best structure the content of the learning solution to account for learners' needs. Chunking refers to combining relevant information into blocks that are easier to absorb.

For example, you could design some microlearning content that takes no more than 10–15 minutes to introduce a concept, contextualize it in practice, and offer instructions for applying it on the job. You could also include activities, such as reflection periods, where learners are presented with a concept and an application activity, followed by a period where they are asked to reflect on the outcome or to identify situations that parallel the new behavior in their day-to-day life.

Mnemonic Devices

Mnemonic devices aid in the retention and retrieval of information from memory and can include such things as acronyms, models, images, infographics, and rhyming devices. In designing your solutions, look for sticky, memorable, visual ways to represent your content. Mnemonic devices support Capacity as they reduce the cognitive load needed by the learner to process and recall the relevant content.

Operations Calendar

The operations calendar is less of a direct design device than it is a planning device when thinking through the scheduling and launch of your solutions. Regarding Capacity, it is critical to take into account the other enterprise and role-specific activities your learners may be facing when you want to deploy your learning programs. For example, launching sales training at the end of a sales period is likely to result in no one completing the activities, or doing so with a minimum of attention while they are focused on doing their jobs. Taking things like this into account when planning can go a long way to successful learning solution design when thinking through structural components and timing of design elements in complex and extended learning journeys.

How to Integrate Layering When Designing Solutions

The Layering domain of CLICS focuses on the necessary sequencing of the concepts contained within the solution and how that solution then conceptually builds from and to other learning elements the learners need to know as part of a longer learning journey. This requires becoming familiar with the learners' job roles, learning paths, or curricula. Ultimately, it comes down to integrating any broader constructs that will help you determine how building blocks will come together and how the flow of information will be presented so the learners can make sense of the new information.

Layering analysis often results in a recommended list of topics or objectives that surround the new behaviors and skills for the learner needs. It typically reveals role-specific behaviors and skills learners either already have or will need to learn in the future. This list then would be sequenced into a logical and necessary order such that each concept builds on the ones before and lays the groundwork for those that come after.

To this end, these are two techniques to employ when designing the solution:

- Context mapping
- Deliberate practice and repetitious exposure

Context Mapping

The context mapping technique shows up in the design of the learning solution as a concept flow that identifies the dependencies between concepts. This mapping usually shows up in high-level and detailed design documents as a means of keeping the necessary sequencing of learning objectives and associated concepts. Additionally, high-level designs should identify other learning elements aligned to relevant learner populations, which are in turn used to place the solution where appropriate in that broader path or curriculum for learners.

Deliberate Practice and Repetitious Exposure

Deliberate practice and repetitious exposure address the challenge that learning does not happen through single exposure to concepts. Learning happens over time as learners have opportunities to practice and fail, reflect, practice and get it right, reflect, and repeat. This technique tends to show up in design as the intentional inclusion of repeated opportunities for application of the relevant behaviors, opportunities for feedback, and access to role models to envision the desired behaviors.

How to Integrate Intrinsic Enablers When Designing Solutions

The Intrinsic enablers domain of CLICS focuses on understanding what about the requested solution will appeal to the learners. This requires understanding the learners' current state versus future state and how closing that gap might be appealing to them. Additionally, the workplace considerations for this domain require connecting the learner value proposition to an understanding of what must exist in the environment to support and reinforce the solution.

The needs analysis should yield information about the pertinent learner population and what they will potentially find motivating and valuable. Creating a successful solution then becomes a design exercise that focuses the learners on the value of learning the new behaviors and skills. Learners will feel intrinsically motivated when something makes them feel more competent and connected, or offers a greater sense of autonomy. Think of it as flipping the switch so that learners want to learn (they are pulled) rather than feel like they have to learn (they are pushed); it is finding out how to ignite the learners' engagement or passion.

To this end, some design techniques to employ include leveraging intrinsic and extrinsic motivational approaches through:

- Communications
- Points or rewards
- Experiential activities

These techniques can be leveraged both in the formal content and the marketing and rollout of the new solution.

Communications

While communications are not usually a part of the formal learning content, they can serve as a powerful tool to drive learner engagement and motivation when used appropriately. Expanding on traditional logistical communications, this technique is all about the thoughtful inclusion of messaging and positioning of essential points intended to nudge, encourage, explain, position, and highlight the motivating factors that will appeal to the learner.

Points or Rewards

Points or rewards can be used as reinforcements to motivate learners. These typically surface as badges or leaderboards, providing a sense of confidence and competence when they are completed, as well as bursts of motivation on learning journeys to stay on the path to completion. They can be either public or private.

Experiential Activities

Using experiential activities can build in complexity and enable small successes to grow to large successes, helping learners develop greater confidence in their competence and drive their intrinsic motivation to see the learning experience through to the end. An example of experiential learning would be interactive role-playing with feedback or a collaborative simulation where behaviors and knowledge are applied in action as a practice activity. Both provide an opportunity to actively apply concepts while getting a sense of what works and what doesn't.

How to Integrate Coherence When Designing Solutions

The Coherence domain of CLICS focuses on understanding if the solution's concepts make sense with each other, and how and if the solution as a whole fits with existing behaviors and within the current operating environment.

The needs analysis of Coherence helps to define just how large a cognitive or behavioral gap the learner will need to close to successfully learn and adopt the behaviors and understanding defined as part of the solution.

Here are some techniques to employ when designing a coherent solution:

- Draw parallels to existing understanding
- Promote cognitive and visual fluency

Draw Parallels to Existing Understanding

Drawing parallels in a learning solution design creates a cognitive contextual map that learners can use to build the associated networks necessary to integrate new information. This directly connects concepts that the learner already understands to the new behaviors. Additionally, this technique, when employed properly in your learning designs, can also aid the Capacity domain by minimizing the cognitive load requirements on learners to assimilate the introduced concepts.

For example, when you are introducing new behaviors or concepts in your design, be sure to include examples of how the behavior compares to current behaviors. With new concepts, you can explain how that concept is related to, builds on, or extends some information learners already know. This is particularly useful in software application training, where you may be teaching a new procedure. When explaining how that procedure works, relate it to a procedure the learner is likely to know from past learning interventions, or even earlier in the current learning.

Promote Cognitive and Visual Fluency

Cognitive and visual fluency serves double duty, aiding both Coherence and Capacity requirements. It has to do specifically with how simply and attractively you can convey concepts and behavioral goals and objectives (minimize cognitive dissonance) while also minimizing the amount of cognitive load on your learners.

An example of cognitive and visual fluency would be laying out very technical details and statistics in an attractively designed infographic that tells the learner a visual story. This presentation is likely to make much more sense, and be far more memorable, than a table of raw data. It's the difference between a text filled with numbers versus an attractive looking pie chart or scatter plot with key points highlighted to show the learner where to focus.

How to Integrate Social Connections When Designing Solutions

The Social connections domain of CLICS focuses on how new behaviors will be supported and reinforced by others in the environment surrounding the learners.

The needs analysis considerations for this domain should provide a solid understanding of what good performance looks like. A useful analysis should also identify what support will exist within the environment to provide feedback and reinforcement. This might include peers, experts, or managers and leaders equipped to act as both role models and coaches to reinforce the learning of the solution.

To this end, some techniques to employ when designing the solution include activating or tapping into the social network of behavioral learning via:

- Feedback and modeling
- Performance support

Each of these can show up in the learning design of a solution as tangible learning activities or resources.

Feedback and Modeling

With the feedback and modeling technique, the goal is to incorporate identified networks of learners, role models, and experts into the design of your learning solution, alongside the practice and repetition activities (from the Layering domain). The desired outcome is that learners will have access to feedback from others who can observe their demonstration of the relevant behaviors in action to understand if they are getting it or not. Additionally, being able to observe role models can provide valuable context and examples of what good looks like to guide the learners' own demonstration of the behaviors at the relevant points.

Performance Support

In addition to the formal learning experience that you design around requested learning solutions, we now understand how equally important access to support information is in the flow of work. This will typically show up in learning designs as microlearning practice activities or knowledge nuggets assigned at regular intervals following a more formal learning program. These microbursts of learning are aimed at sustaining the desired behaviors and skills. Another support resource would be videos of relevant behaviors being performed depending on what the behaviors might be.

Looking Ahead

CLICS is applicable no matter what approach your organization chooses to use in serving your learners. The popular instructional design methodologies in use today, such as ADDIE, SAM, and Agile, focus on the design methods rather than the content that should be included in the solution. While there are steps and tasks related to creating learning objectives, they do not tell you how to define learning objectives. The power of design thinking, and by extension CLICS, enables a more human-centered approach to learning.

Specifically, these are the key principles of strong analysis that lead to strong design and development:

- Focusing on the learner first
- Leveraging behavioral science insights to shape how we approach learning
- Guiding business leaders to make more human-centric decisions and plans
- Increasing the likelihood of learning that lasts through science-based analysis

CHAPTER 10
The Future of Workplace Learning

As we reflect on what we've learned, we've challenged ourselves to better understand the purpose of analysis in solving learning and workplace problems, and how all this positions us for the future. This book has been a catalyst to understand the changing nature of work. For us, three fundamental shifts have changed both the way we work and the way we live—a shift in integration, a shift in decision making, and a shift in meaning.

A Shift in Integration

Our expectations of work have been rebalanced within the broader context of our lives. While the idea of work-life balance has been around for some time, the meaning has shifted to work-life integration. The combination of a global pandemic, shifting workforce demographics, the acceleration of digitization, global warming, and social unrest have fueled the need for a rebalancing. Previously, balance was an attempt to compartmentalize work and life in both time and space. But the pandemic blew that construct apart, and life took a global center stage in ways we had never experienced collectively before. The messiness and chaos of living was on full display for all to see—and it shattered the artificial wall between work and life. Today, it almost seems absurd to think about how much energy we've historically invested in creating this artificial distinction.

A Shift in Decision Making

Our need for choice and flexibility is real, and our decisions have become more deliberate. Along with rebalancing comes the increased responsibility for planning and becoming more purposeful in our decisions. Reorienting ourselves to hybrid work as the norm means rethinking just about everything, both for individuals and organizations.

Employee experiences (EX) are being redesigned to address five core elements: when I work, where I work, how I work, with whom I work, and why I work. Each of these EX elements requires decisions on the part of the individual, team, and larger organization. And the most striking dynamic is these decisions cannot be made in isolation from one another. To foster a successful hybrid work environment requires more communication and more agility than legacy virtual environments. Our long-standing assumptions about the value of an office as a physical destination have been called into question. At the same time, our awareness of our need for social connectedness and personal relationships has never been greater. Creating new work environments that blend the best of virtual with the best of in-office to create a new category of purposeful, hybrid work is the transformation under way.

A Shift in Meaning

Our humanity is core to happiness.

Perhaps this may be the most important and lasting shift we are experiencing, as it is a shift in values. Programs about well-being, mindfulness, and stress reduction were the pre-pandemic warning signs that something needed to change. The saying, "Change doesn't happen until the pain of staying the same exceeds the pain of making a change" certainly applies to the world of work. The volume and acceleration of information and technology over the last several decades reached an unsustainable tipping point. We're not computers, we're humans. It's time to embrace our humanity—with all the insights, emotions, joys, and challenges that brings—by making work a more robust and engaging place to invest our limited time.

How Do These Shifts Impact Workplace Learning?

Current-day industry research points to rapidly changing employee expectations, which in turn are challenging companies to rethink their employment brand and employee value proposition. The desire for greater choice and flexibility is likely here to stay, impacting when, how, and where learning is consumed. Learning can be a powerful vehicle to foster lasting professional relationships within organizations, the kind of relationships that create strong bonds between individuals and with the organization itself. Industry research consistently shows a strong correlation between investing in talent development and the increased strength of cultural norms as well as higher levels of engagement. So-called soft skills, such as demonstrating empathy, building trust, and collaboration, are no longer considered discretionary, but are now seen as critical capabilities. In short, the role of learning has a golden opportunity to support rebalancing life, enabling choice, and fostering meaning at work.

Our Call to Action: Make Learning More Human-Centric

Behavioral science relies on empirical data that informs our understanding about how humans think, feel, behave, and communicate. To achieve lasting learning, we believe it all starts with understanding human psychology—how people process, retain, and apply learning in their everyday work environments. Without factoring in these realities, behavior change at scale will remain unnecessarily difficult. The long-standing push to promote organizational rather than behavioral science as the solution to human problems is flawed, as it relies on big data, market trends, and the "wisdom" of the crowd. While all these data sources can be useful, they ignore the role and impact of the human brain. The fields of social science and neuroscience are bridging the gap between organizational instincts and human behaviors. Applying social science insights to the world of work is a predictable path to achieving behavior change at scale. Once we appreciate how our brains learn, our ability to conduct a CLICS analysis can promote giant leaps forward, ensuring learning that lasts.

Acknowledgments

Thank you to the uniquely talented and generous individuals who contributed their time and expertise to the development of our ideas. Your insights made this book a richer experience not only for the authors, but more importantly for our readers.

From the world of business and workplace learning:
- Brandon Carson
- Jesse Jackson
- Kimo Kippen
- Kelly Palmer
- Steven Sitek

From the world of research and university learning:
- Adam Alter, PhD
- Lisa Son, PhD
- Tessa West, PhD
- Paul Zak, PhD
- Jamil Zaki, PhD

And of course, thanks to the publishing and editorial team at ATD Press, as well as the ATD team and community at large; your professionalism and guidance was superb. You challenged our thinking, clarified our ideas and accelerated our success. Thank you for your confidence in us.

A Brief Tutorial on the Science of Testing Programs

Is this tutorial for you? Possibly, possibly not. Many learning professionals are keen to answer this question—"Did your program or initiative make an impact?"—so they can promote the change that they wish to see in their organization, justify their spending and budget, and plan on other supplements that are needed to keep developing and upskilling employees.

The approach to measurement is fraught with frustration because the process to measure effectively is daunting—isolating causes is difficult work for many reasons, including experience in conducting experiments, defining the parameters, and isolating the control group.

Thus, many learning professionals fall prey to the trap of assuming causation from correlational data, which causes deep concerns for future plans and strategy. And, even if there is the ability and will to apply a rigorous approach to measurement, it can be fairly difficult to do so when there are complicated organizational partnerships and collaborations that need to be in place first (for example, the need to set up relevant control groups and how "messy" that is in a corporate setting, especially while other business leaders rarely consider this or view it as a priority). Not many are willing or able to implement such an approach.

This appendix is here to help you if:

- You are a learning professional who wants to apply a rigorous approach to measurement and assessment.
- You are asked to justify a rigorous approach to assessment in preparation for a dialogue with business leaders.

Correlation ≠ Causation!

Imagine you are using a training program to increase sales. You implement this program to a select group of senior sales members. After six months, you hand out a survey and find that those who went through the training report having higher-quality sales conversations. You conclude that the training directly influenced sales, so you advise senior leaders to invest in implementing this training program throughout the organization.

Was this the right decision?

Before answering this question, let's define some terms. *Correlation* means that an association, or a relationship, exists between two or more variables (such as a training program and sales increase), but this association does not directly imply cause and effect (for example, that the training program caused a sales increase). All it means is that when one variable changes, so does the other. The training correlates with the sales increase.

However, this is where so many learning professionals fall prey to the "correlation trap"—even though a relationship exists between the training and sales increase, it does not necessarily mean that the training caused the sales impact. This relationship could have some other factor, a confounding variable, that is causing the relationship between training and the sales increase. Although it seems the training program directly influenced sales, it could be that the caliber of the group, such as senior sales members, or the combination of other training this group received is what is driving the increase in sales.

The only way to claim a causal relationship between variables is to directly test them via an experiment using the scientific method.

 Research Basis: How Correlations Are Quantified

The magnitude or strength of the correlation and the direction of that relationship is indicated by the correlation coefficient, represented by the letter *r* statistically, and can range from -1 to +1. More strongly correlated variables will have a correlation coefficient of +1 or -1 but weakly associated variables will have a correlation closer to zero. A stronger correlation indicates that a change in one variable will predictably affect changes in the other variable.

- Weak correlations are -0.3 / +0.3
- Moderate correlations are -0.5 / +0.5
- Strong correlations are -0.7 / +0.7

The sign of the correlation indicates the direction of the relationship—either positive or negative.

- **A positive correlation** means that the variables move in the same direction. As one variable goes up or increases, so does the other. For example, as engagement in the company goes up, so do productivity and revenue growth.
- **A negative correlation** means that the variables are inversely related. As one variable goes down or decreases, the other variable goes up or increases. For example, as engagement in the company goes up, absenteeism and presenteeism in the organization go down.

Approach Measurement via the Scientific Method

Using the scientific method to understand the impact of a program is crucial because it is the basis of navigating data complexity. When we don't rely on scientific methodology, we can only rely on the wisdom of the crowd, personal intuition, or guesswork. While none of these sources are "bad" or completely unreliable, there are many examples in history to suggest they are not infallible or error-free—we need evidence to support claims. It is only through systematic scientific research that we can gain an objective understanding of data and measurements rather than relying on preconceived notions and assumptions.

Develop a Theory and Hypothesis

The basic premise of the scientific method is starting with an initial idea (having a theory and hypothesis), then testing that idea in the organization (in the form of empirical observations). Landing on the idea is important because if we don't know the type of question we want to answer then what data are we collecting and why? Testing and collecting empirical observations can lead to further ideas that are continually tested and reiterated and so on. In this way, we can consider the scientific process as circular and iterative (Figure A-1).

Figure A-1. The Scientific Processs

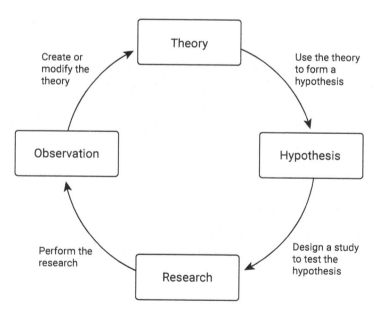

The scientific process involves a circular process of stating a theory, testing the relevant hypothesis, conducting research, and modifying the theory based on findings.

One thing learning professionals should be aware of is that a theory and a hypothesis are two different types of ideas. Knowing the difference has implications for how we design our experiment to test our ideas. Their definitions follow:

- **A theory** is a broad idea that proposes an explanation for an observed event. It is usually complex and vague and difficult to test or measure. For example, we might have a theory that our sales team is weak and has a talent problem or they need training to upskill their capabilities to drive sales. These are all reasonable to consider but too complex to be tested all at once. Instead, we can focus on one aspect of our theory to test.
- **A hypothesis** is a testable prediction about our theory—what do we expect to see and why? It is difficult to properly test our talent density issue in sales if we fire the entire team and start fresh. But, we can focus on implementing a training program to help upskill capabilities—this creates the opportunity for a hypothesis that is testable and measurable.

Test Your Hypothesis and Collect Data

Once we have decided on our hypothesis, we can go out and collect data to test. There are different ways to collect data:

- Interviews, case studies, or focus groups
- Surveys

Interviews, Case Studies, or Focus Groups

Interviews are where we talk with a person, or a few individuals, in depth to collect what is known as qualitative data. Qualitative data can be broadly understood as descriptive, prose-based information.

- **Pro:** Focusing on one or few individuals; provides extremely rich information.
- **Con:** Although data richness is provided, the data is hard to generalize to others. Generalizing means being able to apply the findings to others in the organization.

Surveys

Surveys are questions answered by participants, usually administered in the form of questionnaires to gain quantitative data. Quantitative data is typically numerically based, such as responses on a Likert scale.

- **Pro:** Depending on the length of a survey, it can be completed in a relatively short time so it can be easily distributed to a large number of people at once. This allows the researcher to sample the population in a quick and efficient way.
- **Con:** Unlike interview methods, surveys allow for generalization since the data is collected beyond a handful of individuals. However, if the sample who responded was not representative of the larger population, the data might be biased. This means if we sent out an engagement survey to an organization of 10,000

employees but only 100 responded, all from the same department, this data not only had a low response rate (only 1 percent) but also selected responses from those in one group.

Analyze and Interpret Findings

We can test, through experimentation, by following the steps outlined here. Testing via an experiment can be time-consuming, so a lot of learning professionals tend not to engage, but experiments can provide a lot of information and a more accurate understanding of data. The more decisions you can make based on scientific analysis, the less your work will be based on hunches or rumors.

These are the essential components of experiment testing, which I refer to as the STAR method:
- Specify your hypothesis
- Test two groups (experimental versus control group)
- Assign a representative sample randomly to experimental or control groups
- Review results; repeat

Specify Your Hypothesis

Experimenting starts with having a clear and specific hypothesis. Hypotheses can be formulated by our observations of what is happening in the organization. In this case, we want to test if a certain training program will directly influence sales.

Test Two Groups

We should aim to have two groups to test: the experimental group and the control. These two groups should be designed to be the same except for one difference—the training program. The experimental group should receive the training program. The control group should not. Because the program is the only difference between these groups, whatever results that are obtained can be attributed to this difference rather than anything else.

In an experiment, what we are attempting to uncover is whether the change in one thing affects or causes a change in another. Here, it is important to know the main two variables that are affected:
- The **independent variable** is what has been manipulated or affected by the experimenter—in this case, the training program.
- The **dependent variable** is the outcome or the effect of the independent variable—in this case, how much learning has happened.

It is crucial to clearly define these variables before conducting an experiment so any differences can be clearly understood.

Assign a Representative Sample of the Population Randomly to One of These Two Groups

Whom we collect data from is just as important as the way in which we collect data. If we are looking to understand how to increase engagement in the organization, how and whom we survey are critical to help us interpret the data accurately. The first step is to collect data from a representative sample from the population. A representative sample is a smaller group from the larger population (if we imagine the whole organization) in which every demographic category from the larger population is represented proportionally. So, if we are interested in testing whether a certain program increases engagement in the organization, we need to include a representative sample of participants into the experiment—those in sales, operations, marketing, finance, and so forth. If we only test using one department, managers in IT, then the data collected will be biased or skewed to their experience and will not reflect others' experience as a whole.

Once a representative sample is selected, we ensure that we randomly assign each member to either the experimental group or the control group. We want to ensure that there are not any inherent group differences from the start even before applying the program. For example, using our sales example, we need to make sure that senior members of the sales team are not the only ones receiving training, while the junior members are placed in the control condition. We need to ensure a strong mix of both types of levels in both groups to eliminate confounding variables.

Review Results; Repeat

Are the results clear regarding our hypothesis?

Once we collect data and analyze the group differences, the key is to review the findings, interpret what makes sense, then repeat the experiment if needed. It might be helpful to test the hypothesis with another sample in the population (for example, another regional center) to see if we receive the same results.

In the end, the goal of assessment is to have clear results and be able to generalize the findings to a larger population, thereby giving us more clarity on how to invest our time and resources.

References

Alter, A.L., and D.M. Oppenheimer. 2009. "Uniting the Tribes of Fluency to Form a Metacognitive Nation." *Personality and Social Psychology Review* 13(3): 219–235. doi.org/10.1177/1088868309341564.

Bellezza, F.S. 1981. "Mnemonic Devices: Classification, Characteristics and Criteria." *Review of Educational Research* 51:247–275.

Berkowitz, A.D. 2004. *The Social Norms Approach: Theory, Research, and Annotated Bibliography*. Whitepaper, August. alanberkowitz.com/articles/social_norms.pdf.

Bodie, G.D., W.G. Powers, and M. Fitch-Hauser. 2006. "Chunking, Priming, and Active Learning: Toward an Innovative Approach to Teaching Communication-Related Skills." *Interactive Learning Environment* 14(2): 119–135.

Bransford, J.D., A.L. Brown, and R. Cocking. 2000. *How People Learn*. Washington, DC: National Academy Press.

Bruner, J.S. 1977. *The Process of Education*. Cambridge, MA: Harvard University Press.

Burg, N. 2018. "Diversity and Inclusion: What's the Difference, and How Can We Ensure Both?" *Forbes*, June 25. forbes .com/sites/adp/2018/06/25/diversity-and-inclusion-whats-the-difference-and-how-can-we-ensure-both.

Chi, M.T.H., P. Feltovich, and R. Glaser. 1981. "Categorization and Representation of Physics Problems by Experts and Novices." *Cognitive Science* 5:121–152.

Collins, A.M., and E.F. Loftus. 1975. "A Spreading-Activation Theory of Semantic Processing." *Psychological Review* 82(6): 407–428. doi.org/10.1037/0033-295X.82.6.407.

Dasgupta, N. 2011. "Ingroup Experts and Peers as Social Vaccines Who Inoculate the Self-Concept: The Stereotype Inoculation Model." *Psychological Inquiry* 22(4): 231–246. doi.org/10.1080/1047840X.2011.607313.

Deutsch, M., and H. Gerard. 1955. "A Study of Normative and Informational Social Influences Upon Individual Judgment." *Journal of Abnormal and Social Psychology* 51:629–636.

Dweck, C.S. 2007. *Mindset: The New Psychology of Success*. New York: Ballantine Books.

Ebbinghaus, H. 1885. *Memory: A Contribution to Experimental Psychology*. New York: Dover.

Egan, D.E., and B.J. Schwartz. 1979. "Chunking in Recall of Symbolic Drawings." *Memory & Cognition* 7:149–158. doi.org/10.3758/BF03197595.

Ehrlich, K., and E. Soloway. 1984. "An Empirical Investigation of the Tacit Plan Knowledge in Programming." In *Human Factors in Computer Systems*, edited by J.C. Thomas. Norwood, NJ: Ablex.

Ericsson, K.A., R.T. Krampe, and C. Tesch-Römer. 1993. "The Role of Deliberate Practice in the Acquisition of Expert Performance." *Psychological Review* 100(3): 363–406. doi.org/10.1037/0033-295X.100.3.363.

Hammerness, K. 2006. "From Coherence in Theory to Coherence in Practice." *Teachers College Record* 108:1241–1265.

Larkin, J.H., J. McDermott, D. Simon, and H. Simon. 1980. "Expert and Novice Performance in Solving Physics Problems." *Science* 208:1335–1342.

Larkin, J.H. 1981. "Enriching Formal Knowledge: A Model for Learning to Solve Problems in Physics." In *Cognitive Skills and Their Acquisition*, edited by J.R. Anderson. Hillsdale, NJ: Erlbaum.

Larkin, J.H. 1983. "The Role of Problem Representation in Physics." In *Mental Models*, edited by D. Gentner and A.L. Stevens. Hillsdale, NJ: Erlbaum.

Larkin, J.H., and H.A. Simon. 1987. "Why a Diagram Is (Sometimes) Worth Ten Thousand Words." *Cognitive Science* 11(1): 65–100. doi.org/10.1016/S0364-0213(87)80026-5.

Lesgold, A. 1988. "Problem solving." In *The Psychology of Human Thought*, edited by R.J. Sternberg and E.E. Smith. Cambridge, UK: Cambridge University Press.

Mayer, R.E. 2002. "Multimedia Learning." *The Annual Report of Educational Psychology in Japan* 41:27–29.

Miller, G.A. 1956. "The Magical Number Seven, Plus or Minus Two: Some Limits on Our Capacity for Processing Information." *Psychological Review* 68:81–87.

Simon, D.P., and H.A. Simon. 1978. "Individual Differences in Solving Physics Problems." In *Children's Thinking: What Develops?*, edited by R. S. Siegler. Mahwah, NJ: Lawrence Erlbaum Associates.

Stadtfeld, C., A. Vörös, T. Elmer, Z. Boda, and I.J. Raabe. 2019. "Integration in Emerging Social Networks Explains Academic Failure and Success." *Proceedings of the National Academy of Sciences* 116(3): 792–797. pnas.org/content/116/3/792.

Sweller, J. 1988. "Cognitive Load During Problem Solving: Effects on Learning." *Cognitive Science* 12(2): 257–285. doi:10.1207/s15516709cog1202_4.

Threlkeld, K. 2021. "Employee Burnout Report: COVID-19's Impact and 3 Strategies to Curb It." *Indeed*, March 11. indeed.com/lead/preventing-employee-burnout-report.

Tigner, R.B. 1999. "Putting Memory Research to Good Use." *College Teaching* 47(4): 149–152.

Yerkes, R.M., and J.D. Dodson. 1908. "The Relation of Strength of Stimulus to Rapidity of Habit-Formation." *Journal of Comparative Neurology and Psychology* 18:459–482. doi:10.1002/cne.920180503.

Index

Page numbers followed by *f* and *t* refer to figures and tables, respectively.

About the Authors

Janet N. Ahn

Janet Ahn, PhD, is an experienced experimental social psychologist preparing some of the world's biggest organizations for the challenges of tomorrow. She believes in the power of behavioral science to transform lives and companies. She trained with eminent psychologists from Barnard College, Columbia University (Bachelor degree), New York University (PhD), and Teachers College, Columbia University (postdoctoral fellowship).

She spent more than 12 years in higher education as a tenure-track professor of psychology, and built a portfolio of consulting, teaching, and research expertise in behavior change, motivation and persistence, goal pursuit, growth mindset, cognitive biases, inter- and intra-group dynamics, survey methods and assessment, experimental methods, statistics, and design. As a global organizational leader, she leads product innovation, research and development, and digital solutions expansion on topics such as how leaders can effectively manage teams in a hybrid workplace, organizational responsibility for individual employee well-being, management and leadership development, and diversity, equity, and inclusion. She is a sought-after speaker and subject matter expert at academic and industry conferences. Her work has also been featured in various media outlets such as *Axios*, *Women's Health Magazine*, *Thrive Global*, NPR, *American Educator*, *Business Insider*, CBS, and *USA Today*.

Janet is a first-generation college student and is bilingual in Korean and English. Her hobbies include staying active by hiking, biking, and practicing yoga. She lives in the Atlanta area with her husband and two daughters.

Mary F. Slaughter

Mary F. Slaughter is a seasoned corporate executive, human capital consultant, and published author. Her global enterprise roles have included chief learning officer, chief talent officer, global head of employee experience, chief diversity and inclusion officer, and chief human resources officer. In addition to consulting with Fortune 100 firms on their talent agendas, Mary has worked for such notable brands as AT&T, Lucent Technologies, Wachovia, SunTrust, Morningstar, The NeuroLeadership Institute, Deloitte, and EY. Her executive advisory roles have including the Association for Talent Development (ATD) Board of

Directors, Bersin by Deloitte's Advisory Council, and The Conference Board's Council on Learning, Development and Organizational Performance. She also has specialized in advising women CEOs leading start-ups in Silicon Valley.

A frequent industry speaker, Mary has been featured in *Harvard Business Review, Business Insider,* PwC's *strategy+business, Fast Company, Quartz, Reworked, Talent Management, TD, CLO, Selling Power,* and *Consulting* magazines.

Under her leadership, her teams have won awards from Bersin & Associates for leadership development, Brandon Hall for sales talent management, *CLO Magazine* for academic partnerships, *Training Magazine's* Top 125, ATD BEST for exceptional enterprise learning, and *Consulting Magazine* as one of the top management consulting firms for building a career.

Mary resides in Atlanta with her amazing daughters who brighten her life every day.

Jon Thompson

Jon has spent the past 25+ years serving clients, stakeholders, and learners in the talent development space. He has held roles at organizations of all sizes, from startups to global corporations, both in industry and in service, as an internal and external consultant with organizations such as IBM, SunTrust Banks, Deloitte, The NeuroLeadership Institute, EY, and The Coca-Cola Company, where he currently serves as director of learning experience and innovation. Additionally, Jon served four years in leadership positions with the Greater Atlanta Chapter of ATD, including two years as the VP of technology on the chapter's executive board. He also has been part of two ATD BEST and Training Top 125 award-winning teams.

Jon has a passion for learning strategy, technology, and architecture, especially as it relates to the continuous learning model and the intersection of ways in which technology both supports and enables effective behavior change and meaningful learning experiences for learners.

Jon lives in the Atlanta area with his wife, their two daughters, and two dogs.